MONETARY REFORM AND THE PRICE OF GOLD

MONETARY REFORM AND

THE PRICE OF GOLD

ALTERNATIVE APPROACHES

EDITED BY RANDALL HINSHAW

96916

THE JOHNS HOPKINS PRESS: BALTIMORE

FOREWORD

The Bologna Center Conference on Gold and International Monetary Reform, from which this book originates, was assembled at the European outpost of The Johns Hopkins University's School of Advanced International Studies in Bologna, Italy, during mid-January, 1967. Both the time and place of meeting were elements contributing to its liveliness and success. A few months previously, accumulating evidence began to reveal disturbing trends in international monetary reserves which lent a new urgency to the search for an acceptable solution to the vexatious problem of international monetary reform. The dialogue among contending exponents of reform took on a sharper tone on both sides of the Atlantic and, at the level of officialdom at least, became more and more deeply tinged by national preoccupations. The Bologna Center, with its mixed graduate student body and faculty of Europeans and Americans, which reacts as a sensitive barometer to such changing pressures in the international environment, provided the kind of setting and intellectual atmosphere which were conducive to reasoned and lively argument and debate among the experts who had been brought together.

The conference developed according to a plan which, if not altogether unique, differed substantially from the pattern customarily followed in recent years. No papers were reproduced and made available to all participants in advance. Instead, five distinguished men were asked to speak formally, with or without previously prepared manuscripts, and then to confront each other in open dialogue in the presence of their peers. Three of these (Edward M. Bernstein, Jacques Rueff, and Robert Triffin) are major protagonists of differing schools of thought on the question of international monetary reform; one (Milton Gilbert) is a leading technician whose hand is on the pulse beat of the international monetary system; and the last (Lord Robbins) is one of the greatest living economists, respected and esteemed throughout the world for his wisdom no less than for the qualities of his scholarship. It was Lord Robbins who set the tone of the conference in his introduction to the discussion and who, by his presence no less than through his interventions, held it throughout to the highest level of objectivity.

The idea of the conference emerged at a simple luncheon in February, 1966, following a seminar which Professor Randall Hinshaw had organized at the Bologna Center. The guest on this occasion was Philip Cortney, known to everyone who has concerned himself seriously with international monetary problems. His remarks in the seminar had been so provocative of discussion among Center students and faculty that someone at the luncheon suggested the desirability of bringing together the major protagonists of international monetary reform for open dialogue and debate. Mr. Cortney was attracted to this idea and in the next few months the decision was reached to try to do just that. In fact, by July, 1966, the main lines of the conference were already set and from that time on Mr. Cortney and Professor Hinshaw labored indefatigably to bring it to fruition. The debt of gratitude owing to both of these men is very great indeed.

Without Mr. Philip Cortney there would have been no conference such as this. It was conceived as the result of his stimulating thought and conversation. The grant that the Bologna Center received to finance it came to us as the result of his good offices. But beyond all of this he gave unsparingly of his time and energy to assist in the planning and preparation of the conference every step of the way.

Professor Hinshaw took over the detailed planning of the conference in the summer of 1966 and, with patience and great skill, designed it in all of its details. And when it had come to pass it was he who assumed and executed the important and demanding task of editing this book.

A debt of gratitude is due as well to Mr. Donald H. McLaughlin and Mr. Willard L. Thorp, who jointly chaired the conference and masterfully held it on its course.

Thanks are also certainly due to the members of the Bologna Center staff, who in so many ways, great and small, helped to ensure the smooth functioning of the conference—

especially to Mrs. Gertrude Pellegrini, who, after eleven years at the Center, has become a real professional in conference organization and management.

Miss Carolyn Kelley, a Center student, was of great assistance at various stages in the preparation of the manuscript.

C. GROVE HAINES

Bologna
June 2, 1967

CONTENTS

MONETARY REFORM AND THE PRICE OF GOLD

CHAPTER I

INTRODUCTION

This book is not a conference report. The Bologna Center conference was not conceived as an effort to reach a consensus, and participants were assured in advance that no such effort would be made. Indeed, without this assurance, it would have been impossible to bring together the remarkable group that agreed to participate—a group intentionally selected for its divergent views on policy.

Instead, the purpose of the conference was to probe as deeply as possible into international monetary issues as they now appear—issues that Lord Robbins has aptly described as matters of "appalling intellectual difficulty." In particular, it was hoped that by getting into the same room the authors of the main proposals for reform—Edward M. Bernstein, Jacques Rueff, and Robert Triffin—and by giving them an opportunity not only to restate their positions but to engage in an open dialogue in the presence of other distinguished authorities, the present areas of agreement and disagreement would become clear. This hope was abundantly justified. The dialogue itself is reproduced verbatim as Chapter VII. It revealed a surprising degree of agreement on the diagnosis of present difficulties though not, of course, on policy.

The Bologna Center conference was originally conceived as an effort to explore the future role of gold in international monetary arrangements, with particular attention to the price of gold. As plans for the conference developed, a more ambitious objective took shape: to re-examine the major alternatives in world monetary reform in the light of present circumstances, which in certain important respects are radically different from those of the early 1960s.

The biggest change is that the traditional forms of world monetary reserves are no longer growing. World gold reserves, which throughout the postwar period had been growing at a much lower rate than the gold value of international trade, actually declined in 1966. Despite a record level of gold production, the amount of gold going into hoards and into rapidly expanding industrial uses exceeded the 1966 output. The other main form of reserves—central bank holdings of dollars—also declined in 1966 after growing at a vigorous rate for many years.

The failure of gold and dollar reserves to expand meant two things. For the world as a whole, it gave a new urgency to the problem of providing for an orderly growth of reserves to match the expansion of world production and trade. For the United States, it meant the end of "deficits without tears." Out of a cumulative over-all payments deficit (on an "official reserve transactions" basis) of roughly $20 billion since 1949, the United States had "settled" about half in dollars paid to foreign central banks, and for many individual years the fraction had been much higher than half. As long as this situation persisted, there had been many in the United States who were unimpressed with the need for basic changes in the international monetary system. Indeed, there were some who looked on the dollar-financed deficits as a form of "reverse foreign aid" which provided the United States with total resources somewhat greater than its current income, thus helping, among other things, to preserve U.S. price stability. Their counsel, in effect, was to relax and enjoy the situation and, if possible, to devise inducements to continue it indefinitely. Such an approach, it was argued, would perform a service both for the United States and, by adding to foreign reserves, for the rest of the world.

This brand of thinking—however it may be judged—could play no part in a conference taking place in 1967, for the premises on which it was based no longer corresponded with reality. The era of deficits without tears was over. Indeed, there was the possibility that it might be followed by an era of U.S. external balance, or even surplus, *with* tears. In terms of official reserve transactions, the U.S. balance of payments in 1966 showed a small surplus which, far from inducing an inflow of gold, was accompanied by a gold outflow of over half a billion dollars.

In view of this change in circumstances, it was inevitable that the gold-exchange standard, which has played such a conspicuous role in postwar international finance, should come under close scrutiny. The re-examination was from two points of view: first, in relation to the so-called confidence problem and, second, in relation to the problem of international adjustment. The first problem concerns the gold-exchange standard as an increasingly unstable mechanism—if one wishes to be dramatic, as a house of cards which only a slight jolt might cause to collapse or, to change the metaphor, as a balloon which has been blown so large that it might at any moment burst.

This strand has long been important in the thinking of Robert Triffin and accounts for much, if not most, of his concern with international monetary reform. His proposal for a world central bank, in which the deposits of national central banks would replace existing dollar and sterling reserves, is primarily (though of course not exclusively) designed to deal with the confidence problem.

The same reasoning is also prominent in the thinking of Jacques Rueff. From Rueff's point of view the gold-exchange standard is a malignant growth in the international monetary system; he refers to it as a "cancer." It is an evil, according to Rueff, because of its instability and because it interferes with the mechanism of international adjustment. For both of these reasons Rueff would double the price of gold. Increasing the price of gold would permit the substitution, without deflation, of gold for existing dollar and sterling reserves and, if accompanied by measures to assure a close link between gold and national money supplies, would restore an effective adjustment mechanism.

The attention given to the problem of international adjustment was a conspicuous and unexpected feature of the Bologna Center conference. Participants who expressed views on this subject could be divided into two broad groups, but within each group there were wide divergencies. One group, which included Jacques Rueff, J. E. Meade, John Exter, and Maurice Allais, was concerned with introducing a mechanism that would promote continuous adjustment and thus prevent serious imbalances from emerging. Rueff would do this by restoring the "classical" gold standard—in particular, by re-establishing a close link between gold flows and national money supplies—while Meade would accomplish the same objective by introducing more flexible exchange rates. This group tended to regard the level and growth rate of international reserves as a secondary matter. The other group, which like Rueff favored fixed exchange rates except under conditions of *force majeure,* appeared less concerned with the speed than with the ease and painlessness of adjustment. Both Triffin and Bernstein were in this latter group, with Bernstein making the point that the only reason for discussing reserves is "to make adjustment easier."

Here it is easy to oversimplify, and I may have already done so. Rueff would doubtless argue that continuous adjustment, even with fixed exchange rates, need not be painful, because the payments disequilibria could never become large. Such a system, however, to the extent that it is successful, is highly sensitive to international influences— indeed, that is how it works—and where prices abroad are tending to rise or to fall, continuous adjustment at fixed exchange rates may require considerable domestic price instability. When prices abroad are rising, a country, through no fault of its own, will be under pressure to inflate, and when prices abroad are falling, it will be under pressure to deflate. Indeed, with the essentially passive monetary policy implied in this approach, the inflation or deflation will take place automatically and, so long as exchange rates are fixed, can be resisted only by measures which interfere with the adjustment process.

Meade would get around this difficulty by allowing the exchange rate to move up or down. Bernstein and Triffin would get around the difficulty by attaching less importance to continuous adjustment and more importance to the creation of adequate reserves or international credit facilities. They would appear to agree with the point of view expressed elsewhere by Sir Roy Harrod that considerable time may be required for a successful adjustment and that too much emphasis on speed may inflict unnecessary pain.[1] This conclusion is certainly persuasive in cases where the underlying forces are working in the direction of adjustment—for example, in the case of a deficit country that is managing to keep its price level steady while prices abroad are gradually rising. In such a case the best solution may be

---

[1] Sir Roy Harrod, *Reforming the World's Money* (London: Macmillan, 1965), especially Chapter 1.

to provide the country with reserve assistance until the external deficit disappears.

But suppose that long-run influences abroad are of a character which, instead of reducing, increases the disequilibrium—what then? In cases of this kind, reserve support may simply delay and magnify the pain of what Bernstein aptly calls "the most famous of all adjustment processes, the Procrustean bed." Here a change in the exchange rate may be the only satisfactory policy; and one is then led to the question of whether a continuous adjustment by means of a flexible exchange rate would not have been less painful and disruptive. In this connection, it is not relevant to say to Meade that flexible rates are unlikely to work well for a country that is pursuing inflationary policies, since Meade offers his prescription precisely to those countries that are determined to maintain internal price stability (plus high employment and a healthy growth rate) in a world where *other* countries may be pursuing unwise fiscal or monetary policies.

Without taking a stand on this matter, I would like to point out that much of the empirical criticism of fluctuating exchange rates is based on pathological episodes involving war-ravaged economies—notably after World War I.[2] Interesting as this evidence is, it sheds little light on the wisdom of flexible rates for countries which, under more normal conditions, are pursuing internal fiscal and monetary policies aimed at high employment, growth, *and* price stability. A similar comment may be made concerning Robert Triffin's argument against flexible rates in Chapter XI. This argument, which is persuasive within its terms of reference, applies to a country which is *not* pursuing policies directed toward internal price stability but instead is making inflationary or deflationary "mistakes." Accordingly, the argument has little bearing on Meade's analysis, which rests on the assumption that any such mistakes are being made, not at home, but abroad.

To say more would be to encroach unduly on what the members of the conference were superbly able to say for themselves. It may be helpful, however, to indicate briefly

[2] For example, see Ragnar Nurkse's illuminating Chapter V in *International Currency Experience: Lessons of the Interwar Period* (Princeton: League of Nations, 1944).

the plan of the book. The Introduction is followed by the
opening address of Lord Robbins, which is a statement of
the key issues and main alternatives in international monetary evolution. In an admirably balanced and perceptive
way, this paper set the stage for the conference. Next comes
Milton Gilbert's able and highly illuminating description
and analysis of the factual background relating to international liquidity. The ensuing three chapters (IV, V, and VI)
contain the opening statements of Jacques Rueff, Robert
Triffin, and Edward M. Bernstein. These, in effect, are re-
statements of their respective positions as of early 1967.
They are followed by a three-way dialogue among Rueff,
Triffin, and Bernstein which, as indicated earlier, is reproduced verbatim as Chapter VII. In Chapter VIII, Otmar
Emminger gives a most enlightening account of recent
thinking within the Group of Ten, with particular attention
to the question of whether or not to raise the price of gold.
This is followed by a chapter in which three noted gold
experts—William J. Busschau, Donald H. McLaughlin, and
Michael Spieler—give their conclusions regarding the effect
of an increase in the price of gold on world gold reserves,
both through the effect on gold production and through the
effect on gold dishoarding. In Chapter X, seven other conference members, beginning with Professor Meade, present
their views on international monetary reform. The final
chapter opens with Lord Robbins' judicious summary of the
debate as it appeared at the beginning of the closing section.
This summary, in which he presents a number of questions
calling for further illumination, is followed by the concluding statements of Rueff, Bernstein, and Triffin.

CHAPTER II

ISSUES AND ALTERNATIVES

The task which has been assigned to me is to provide some background for the expert discussions that are to follow. For this purpose I propose first to expatiate a little on the general nature of the international monetary problem, then to indicate some salient features of historical antecedents to the present manifestations of that problem, and finally to indulge in certain broad reflections on the main types of solution likely to come under consideration.

I

Let me first enunciate the tremendous platitude that the problem arises from the absence of a common money and a common control of money. There is no single unit in which we may settle our debts and in terms of which we may make our contracts. There is no single body which regulates the purchasing power available, either in a single money or in the different moneys throughout the free-world economy as a whole.

In spite of the excruciating banality of these propositions, I think it is worth while stating them explicitly, since they lead at once to the two leading deficiencies of the present

* In its variety of interests, the career of Lord Robbins suggests that of Lord Keynes. From 1929 to 1961, he was professor of economics at the London School of Economics, where he still lectures. As chairman of *The Financial Times*, he is a leading force in British financial journalism. He is a director of the Royal Opera House, Covent Garden, and a trustee of the National Gallery and of the Tate Gallery. During World War II he headed the Economic Section of the offices of the War Cabinet. He has served as chairman of the Prime Minister's Committee on Higher Education, as president of the Royal Economic Society, and as president of the British Academy. His numerous books include *The Nature and Significance of Economic Science, The Economist in the Twentieth Century, Politics and Economics,* and *The Theory of Economic Policy in Classical Political Economy.*

7

situation: the lack of automatic adjustment at fixed rates of
exchange between expenditure in different areas and the
lack of purposive control of free-world expenditure as a
whole.

The lack of an automatic adjustment mechanism is obvious enough. I am inclined to think, however, that we are
often apt to neglect its most significant implication, namely
that the balance-of-payments difficulties which are such a
persistent feature of the contemporary scene are themselves
essentially difficulties of the exchange markets. Needless to
say, the underlying causes of such difficulties may have their
origin in far wider areas: in changes in money supply either
at home or abroad, in changes in relative costs or demand, in
changes in the currents of saving and investment. But it is
only if there are different monies that these causes manifest
themselves in balance-of-payments difficulties. A common
money does not involve equal rates of growth in all parts of
the monetary area; it does not guarantee the absence of
changes involving positive decline in some parts coexisting
with rapid advance in others; it does not therefore provide
a solvent for all the difficult social problems associated with
such movements. But it does mean, not only by definition
but also because of the actual contrast between internal and
external transactions which we know where it does not
prevail, the absence of special difficulties in the procurement
of special means of payment.

In this connection, I cannot resist quoting David Hume,
whose marvelous essay on the balance of trade, written at
the mid-point of the eighteenth century, contains most of
what we know (or need to know) in this connection:

How is the balance kept in the provinces of every kingdom
among themselves, but by the force of this principle, which makes
it impossible for money to lose its level, and either to rise or sink
beyond the proportion of the labor and commodities which are in
each province? Did not long experience make people easy on this
head, what a fund of gloomy reflections might calculations afford
to a melancholy Yorkshireman, while he computed and magnified
the sums drawn to London by taxes, absentees, commodities, and
found on comparison the opposite articles so much inferior? And
no doubt, had the Heptarchy subsisted in England, the legislature
of each state had been continually alarmed by the fear of a
wrong balance; and as it is probable that the mutual hatred of

these states would have been extremely violent on account of their close neighborhood, they would have loaded and oppressed all commerce, by a jealous and superfluous caution.

Hume was attempting to demonstrate the improbability of balance-of-payments difficulties with what Viner has called simple specie currencies. But he did not neglect to recognize that, once there were independent centers of credit creation in the different national areas, the automatism he was trying to demonstrate ceased to operate.

The absence of common control has more complicated implications. It should go without saying that it precludes an over-all policy regarding aggregate demand. It is conceivable, if the various national authorities focus their financial policies chiefly upon the maintenance of equilibrium in the foreign exchange markets at fixed parities, that even in the absence of common control, they may succeed in achieving this aim. This was indeed the theory—perhaps only a textbook theory—of the classical gold standard. But, unless there is co-ordination, such a focus excludes policies designed to deal with the ups and downs of trade and employment. Convertibility at fixed rates may be maintained. But there may be inflation or deflation throughout the world economy as a whole.

But beyond this, the absence of common control complicates the problem of adjustment itself in a way which is not always fully realized, in that it precludes any clear formulation of rules of the international game. In a system in which there is no *general* inflation or deflation, it is possible to lay down fairly simply rules of this kind. If the balance of payments is negative there should be relative—not necessarily absolute—contraction; if it is positive, the reverse. This simply means that changes in the relative valuations of the various national outputs and services are reflected in relative money flows—in such circumstances it is in fact quite misleading to describe the relative expansion as inflation and the relative contraction as deflation: they are positively equilibrating movements within a general system from which inflation and deflation are absent; and it is a sensible formulation of the rules of the international game to require that they take place.

But now suppose that an unfavorable position of the local balance of payments is due to deflation elsewhere or a favorable movement to inflation of like kind. What are the rules now? Are the authorities of a national area obliged to import deflation or inflation, to contract or expand local prices and incomes, not because of unfavorable or favorable terms in the real condition of international supply and demand, but rather because elsewhere some other authority or authorities are having unwarranted contractions or expansions of their own? My exposition is highly abstract. But I submit that it has had its counterpart in conditions not at all absent from international monetary history since World War I.

At this stage it is necessary to take account of the view that none of this would matter if only the national authorities were prepared to leave their exchanges free to adapt themselves to whatever rates were fixed in the play of international markets. Independent national control of money supply is a fact of life, it is argued. The use of this control to forward all sorts of aims not compatible with fixed rates of exchange is not to be thought out of this world. How much better therefore to recognize this state of affairs; if, instead of creating problems of adjustment by attempting to maintain fixed rates, we let the rates fluctuate freely, all will be well. It is important to realize that not all those who would argue for floating or adjustable rates in particular circumstances—as I would personally—would accept this extreme position: a world in which freely fluctuating rates are an ultimate ideal rather than a *pis aller* in certain emergencies. But it would be a mistake to underestimate the extent of the support which it would receive among some of the most eminent of our contemporaries.

Before dealing with the alleged realism of this proposal, I should like to touch on an ideological aspect. It is sometimes argued that it is an essentially *liberal* solution of our problem—that liberalism relies essentially on the free play of markets; and that, therefore, freely fluctuating exchanges are an essential feature of a world in which there is no common money and no common control. I am often confronted with this argument by friends who imagine that it must be especially congenial to my way of thinking.

I am perfectly prepared to agree that to let an exchange fluctuate rather than to clutter things up with all sorts of special controls is a more liberal policy—if these be the only alternatives. But I am not prepared to admit that a world of fluctuating exchanges is a liberal solution to the international monetary problem. Quite the contrary, indeed; for it should be clear that for such a state of affairs to persist it must be supported by what must surely be regarded as the essentially illiberal practice of prohibiting, or rendering void, contracts in terms of any but the local currency. In a world of fluctuating exchanges, if contracts were genuinely free, they would come to be made more and more in terms of the currency which was expected to fluctuate least; and eventually all monies but one would be eliminated. This is no flight of the theoretical imagination. The tendency to move towards one international money was widely discernible in the days when gold and silver still circulated side by side. And we know that at the present day, were it not for the law, contracts would be made more and more in the currencies expected to be most stable. I certainly would have asked for my academic salary and pension to be paid in dollars or Swiss francs. The whole system of independent national monies rests not on liberty but upon drastic prohibitions. A broad view of the financial history of the last thirty-five years will not fail to emphasize the importance of the legal decisions which invalidated the gold clause in commercial contracts in so many areas.

But, leaving ideology aside, it is clear to me that a general system of freely fluctuating rates between existing national areas is not permanently viable. It is just not on. I will say nothing here of what, to me, are the terrifying inflationary potentialities of such a system. But I do wish to emphasize the inherent improbability of its persistence year in and year out, without a tendency to changes which would involve its abandonment. Please notice that I am *not*—repeat, not—arguing against the device of a floating rate as a temporary substitute for a fixed devaluation of one currency—which in some cases may be preferable. Nor am I denying the possibility of a permanent floating rate between two gigantic world blocs such as the Dollar Area and perhaps Europe, including the Sterling Area. But I do deny the viability of a system in which all, or indeed most, of the existing currencies were free to fluctuate in terms of each other. I deny it in terms of the practicability of working international exchange markets in which there are *no* fixed

guideposts. I deny it still more in terms of the willingness of
the central banks and monetary authorities of the world to
continue to work such a system.

For the fact is that, despite the tendency of governments
to pursue independent internal policies which ultimately
have an internationally disequilibrating tendency, there is
something in the nature of central banking operations
which recoils from the instability of capital values involved
by the existence of fluctuating exchanges. It always seems to
me as if the advocates of this system were using models in
which the various moneys involved were composed exclusively of, say, B. M. Anderson's dodo bones or Marshall's
stock of hard, bright meteoric stones—totally fixed supplies of inconvertible cash with no structure of capital or
credit superadded. Perhaps in such circumstances all would
be well. But these are not the circumstances of the modern
world; and I suggest that if we were to start from scratch
tomorrow, with all the currencies of the world free to fluctuate in terms of each other, it would not be many weeks
before arrangements began to be made for many rates to be
pegged in terms of certain currencies expected to fluctuate
least, with all the problems of maintaining inter-area equilibrium at fixed rates within the larger areas so created.
And it would not be long before the authorities of the larger
areas were reaching out for understandings to maintain
stability of rates between the moneys for which they were
ultimately responsible. We should be back again in our present troubles, each sovereign area with, so to speak, a split
monetary personality, one half with a tendency always to
independent action, one half revolting from the consequences of this tendency.

II

It was to cope with this problem that the present instrument of international co-operation in this sphere, the International Monetary Fund, was planned at the Bretton Woods
Conference in the summer of 1944 and subsequently
brought into existence at the Havana Conference in the
spring of 1946. I shall be criticizing some aspects of this
institution in what I have to say later on. I should therefore
like to say at once that I shall always regard its creation as
one of the most notable manifestations of constructive ideal-

ism in the history of international relations. Perhaps no one who did not actually live through the anxious days and nights of drafting and negotiation at the U.S. Treasury, at Atlantic City, and at Bretton Woods itself, can reconstruct from the dry record of proceedings, and still drier statutes and regulations resulting therefrom, the atmosphere in which it was born. But, as the one surviving member of the U.K. economic delegation, I should like to pay tribute to the drive, the objectivity, and the infinite intellectual resourcefulness of the American authors of the plan and in particular to my dear friend, Edward Bernstein, a true well-wisher for humanity and a great expert if ever there was one.

The leading notions of this plan were twofold: a mobilization of international liquidity and an apparatus for orderly adjustment of exchange rates. The mobilization of international liquidity took the form of quota subscription, determined by a complicated formula designed to take account both of general economic standing and position in world trade, and payable partly in gold, partly in local currencies. Such subscriptions carried with them rights of borrowing money, regulated by various rules which eventually amounted to a normal net limit of 100 per cent of the quota. That it took this form rather than the simpler form of the clearing union proposed by Keynes, with an international money and more drawing rights, was due to the very understandable reluctance of the United States, as representative at that time of the countries with an expectation of a surplus in international trade, to assume unlimited liability for financing other people's overdrafts. Nevertheless, subject to the limitations inherent in this structure, it did afford, for use by members in temporary distress, reinforcements to their reserves of a kind and volume never systematically available before.

As regards provision for orderly adjustment, it must be remembered that it was one of the main objects of the Fund to promote exchange stability. Given the enlarged resources provided by its facilities for drawing, it was hoped that members would be enabled so to manage their affairs that extreme unbalance could be avoided. The facilities were to be regarded not as a license for the pursuit of policies inimical to external equilibrium, but rather as an enlargement of the elbowroom in which to meet unanticipated

causes of unbalance. Yet it was realized that occasions
might arise when this would not be enough, occasions when
equilibrium could only be established at the cost of long-
lasting and damaging contractions; and to meet such contin-
gencies provision was made for alterations of exchange
rates which, being agreed or subject to rule, would not
initiate chain reactions of competitive depreciation. It may
be said with justice that the setting up of the Fund was in a
sense a restoration of a gold standard of sorts. But it was a
gold standard with a difference, with a degree of flexibility
never before contemplated in arrangements of this sort.

Well, it has been a long time since that last night at
Bretton Woods when we were all on our feet waving our
table napkins and cheering as the Russian delegate produced a telegram from Stalin authorizing the signature by
his delegation of the final act of the conference—a signature
which, having regard to subsequent developments, it is perhaps just as well was never honored. It may be a useful
introduction therefore to our discussion of present problems
to ask how far have been fulfilled the high hopes which we
all believed were justified by the success of that conference.
How far have existing institutions provided a solution to the
international monetary problems of the period since World
War II?

If we are trying to establish a perspective, I think the
first thing that must be said is that they have totally failed
to prevent inflation. But this is not surprising. It is an apt
illustration of the chronic tendency of policy to be concerned
with the problems of yesterday rather than tomorrow, that
the prevention of inflation was not on the agenda during all
these discussions. It was the last thing that most of us were
thinking of. There were of course exceptions. I remember
getting up one morning at Bretton Woods to find among my
papers a minute by Sir Ralph (then Mr.) Hawtrey which
had been passed on to me by Keynes. I forget the exact
words of the minute. But the purport was simple. "What's
all this talk about the dangers of deflation?" said the writer;
"*In*flation, not *de*flation, is the postwar problem." "Dear
Lionel," ran Keynes's covering note, "I thought you would
like to see what the old thing is saying. After all, he may be
right." Now I know that there are some who hold that such
falls in the value of money are harmless or even beneficial in

themselves and that the only trouble is their unequal rates and consequent complication of the external adjustment problem. But that is not my view. Quite apart from the cruel distributive injustices involved, the effects on civic virtue and general culture of an economic atmosphere approximating to that of the casino seem to me to be very bad, even if they are often unperceived.

However, I think it must be admitted that there has been very little success in maintaining stable exchange rates. It was perhaps inevitable that, in the period immediately following the war, there should be many alterations. But the war is a long way back; and since then the adjustments which have been thought to be necessary have surely been very much more numerous than was expected or might have been expected at the time. And the chief reason is abundantly clear. There may have been cases where disequilibrium in the foreign exchange market was due to "real" causes—I should like to know more about them. But in the main it has been due to failures of financial policy. National policies of internal expenditure have been such as to *create* conditions of fundamental disequilibrium, and fundamental disequilibrium has occurred. I should like to make it quite clear that I do not oppose adjustment of exchange rates when this state of affairs prevails. All that I am saying is that the frequency of its occurrence in the last fifteen years or so is clear evidence that one of the main objectives of the wartime financial plans has yet to be fully achieved.

Beyond this I submit that experience in this field tends to show that the Fund, constituted as it now is with a largish body of executive directors, chosen at least in part on diplomatic grounds rather than for their standing in the world of international finance, and in continuous telephonic communication with their governments and central banks, is not necessarily a very suitable body for the settlement of such delicate matters as the adjustment of exchange rates. It is no accident that the major devaluations have been agreed (if they have been agreed at all) in more restricted, more informal, consultations. The part played by the official machinery has not been much more than that of a rubber stamp.

I fancy this deficiency is something which is inherent in the nature of the Fund as it is at present and as it is likely in the future to be constituted. It is for this reason that I, personally, have always wished that the postwar monetary reconstruction could have started, as John Williams suggested, on the basis of the restricted membership of the interwar Tripartite Agreement or some such limited body, rather than as the gigantic open club that it is now. I am reasonably clear that such a basis would have been at least as congenial to the United Kingdom as that which was actually adopted. But who were we to oppose our, perhaps cynical, views of the effectiveness of large assemblies to the dedicated idealism of Washington?

When we come to assess the effectiveness of the Fund as a mobilizer of international liquidity, the verdict must be much more complicated. Any complaint that, during the period since the war, the free world as a whole has suffered from a general lack of liquidity seems to me to fail completely in the face of the known facts regarding world inflation. Lack of liquidity in general would have shown itself not in inflationary but in deflationary tendencies. Anyone who urges that during this period we have not had enough inflation, that the governments and central banks of the world have been prevented from desirable expansion for lack of adequate liquidity, should surely have his head examined. During the early stages of the wartime discussions, I, in common with all the other U.K. officials, used to argue passionately in favor of the Keynes plan for a clearing union, which, whatever its other merits or demerits, would certainly have provided more liquidity than the institution which eventually was created; and, at the time, I was disappointed that it had to give way to a more restricted plan. But I must confess that when, during the years which have elapsed, I have asked myself what would have been the outcome had the clearing union been adopted, I have had to admit that it would have been simply—still more inflation.

It may be argued, however, and, I think, argued with reason, that the concept of liquidity which is relevant in this connection is not liquidity in general but international liquidity—the availability of reserves adequate to sustain the convertibility of local currency at fixed rates of exchange. I agree. But I should be prepared to argue that, with one exception—an important exception, I grant—the original resources and regulations of the Fund have not hitherto been inadequate to provide what has been needed. It is not true that there have been cases where the authorities of currencies—areas not in fundamental disequilibrium—have been forced to devalue for lack of adequate assistance to tide over circumstances of special pressure. I could make many criticisms of the structure of the Fund in this respect. Its peculiar constitution as a mixed bag of currencies, only to be sold under very restrictive conditions, brings it about that many of the subscriptions are virtually useless in general mobilization of liquidity. But, even within these limitations, I have yet to learn that for most normal occasions the original resources of the Fund have proved inadequate for the purpose for which they were intended.

The exception of course has been the needs of the United Kingdom in recent years. Here is a case where a major currency area, without being at all in obvious fundamental disequilibrium, has allowed its expenditure at home and abroad to get so out of line with its external earnings as to run into such difficulties in its balance of payments on current account as to arouse widespread alarm concerning its future stability, with the result that its normal reserves and drawing rights have proved inadequate to arrest a dangerous drain. But here, too, is a case where the emergency powers of the Fund to arrange extraordinary borrowing have played a large part in the special operations necessary to restore confidence. It is a case which has already led to some formalization of these emergency powers and, as a result of recent discussions, may lead to still further developments of this kind for the future. I think that it is in the interest of the world at large that arrangements of this sort should exist. But it is hard to make it a reproach to the Fund that emergencies of this sort should have arisen. Rather, blame the financial policy of the country concerned, which on so many occasions since the war has refused to recognize the inevitable damage to the current account of rates of expenditure at home and abroad not warranted by its productivity or its responsibilities in the financial markets of the world.

But the problem does not end here. If it be agreed that, by and large, there has been up to now no shortage of world liquidity and that the powers of the Fund have been adequate, that does not imply that they will be so in the future.

It is perhaps impossible to say a priori what absolute levels
of reserves in the different areas are necessary—so much
depends upon local habit and convention. But it may nevertheless be assumed that, given the existing complex of
habits and conventions, it is desirable, if deflationary pressure is to be avoided, that reserves should increase year by
year in reasonable relation to the growth of production and
trade. Now it seems probable that such an increase is now
no longer guaranteed for the future. Experts may differ in
their quantitative assessment of needs in this respect. But
there seems a reasonable consensus that, in the present
conditions of gold production, industrial demand, and so on,
there is real danger of an insufficient rate of growth in the
future. And to meet this, existing international arrangements are not yet adequate.

Furthermore, there is another danger, potentially even
more menacing. The present reserve arrangements in the
world depend to a very considerable extent on the willingness of many central banks to hold dollars or sterling rather
than gold. If habits should change in this respect: if confidence in either of these key currencies should be so seriously
shaken that there was a simultaneous rush to convert these
holdings into gold, or even if habits and policies should
change not so catastrophically as this, but in such a manner
that many important central banks gradually withdrew the
gold to which these holdings at present entitle them, and
competition for the limited supplies coming forward from
the mines were to be intensified, then the deflationary pressure would be very serious indeed and the pressure to convert might easily develop into a world financial crisis of the
first order of magnitude.

It should be clear therefore that, however effectively the
liquidity requirements of the world at large have been ca-
tered for in the recent past, the future is still latent with
urgent problems which are not likely to be solved by policies
and institutions now operative. It is to some consideration
of the main types of solution which have been suggested
that the last section of my remarks will be directed.

III

Let me say at once that I assume as an axiom that the first
necessity of the contemporary situation is an improvement

in the balance-of-payments situation of the United States and the United Kingdom. While extreme unbalance persists in these quarters it is vain to hope that the authorities of other areas will wish to commit themselves to indefinite support of positions which need to be rectified by domestic action. What is even more relevant, while this unbalance persists, so too must persist that distrust of the key currencies which is one of the most potentially explosive features of the present situation. If it were remedied, I see no reason to suppose that the tendency to substitute gold for key currency holdings, although possibly still present, would be so powerful as to embarrass the course of orderly reform.

But while a removal of the deficits of the key-currency authorities would remove the danger of a catastrophic chain reaction, it would at the same time make even more palpable the need for measures to safeguard the supply of liquidity for the future. For in the recent past, as is well known, the demand for liquidity, in the sense in which I am using the word, has been met at least in part by the supply of key currencies made available by the dollar and sterling deficits. If the areas concerned are henceforth to be in balance or still more if—what for the United Kingdom at least is highly desirable, for local reasons—running a substantial surplus, and if at the same time the supply of new gold for monetary purposes does not increase, then the provision of increasing reserves for the free world as a whole becomes, to that extent, more urgent—though not, of course, as urgent as it would be if confidence in the key currencies were to collapse.

What are the alternative measures proposed to supply these needs? I shall confine myself only to typical schemes and those only in their broadest aspects.

I turn first to proposals which depend upon an alteration of the price of gold. The statutes of the IMF make provision for an alteration of this nature, assuming that it receives the support of the largest powers concerned. It is proposed therefore that advantage be taken of this provision to raise the price by a percentage—there is not complete agreement on the precise amount—sufficient to involve a very substantial increase in the value of existing reserves. At the same time—and this is the spacious and imaginative aspect of these proposals—it is suggested that this increase, or part

of it, be used—either by way of direct repayment or by way
of a spectacular international loan—to liquidate dollar or
sterling claims used as currency reserves, thus substituting
a gold standard old style for the present gold-exchange
standard arrangements.

Let me say at the outset that I find many of the arguments which have been directed against this proposal not a
little unconvincing. Thus I do not think that we rise to the
level of argument appropriate to these momentous questions
if we deny the importance of gold as such, or suggest that
all arguments for a gold standard system rest upon super-
stition or psychopathological fixations. This particular mode
of attack is surely pretty *vieux jeu* nowadays. The theory of
the gold standard—Hume's theory of specie-flow adjustment, Ricardo's theory of the distribution of the precious
metals—may have been incomplete, but it was not just a
meaningless abracadabra: it was a highly sophisticated
analysis designed to show how a world, divided politically
into independent units, might yet enjoy unity in respect of
international economic transactions. And if we turn from
theory to practice, who shall say that on the whole paper
systems have proved superior to gold? Clearly, whatever
hopes we may have for the future—and later on I shall
disclose divergence from the support of gold theory in this
respect—if we are honest we must admit that until now—
with the exception of two deflation periods where the gold
parity had been wrongly fixed—the record of paper systems
is vastly inferior, as regards both internal and external
stability.

If we turn to arguments more specifically directed against
the proposals under discussion, a good deal that is currently
said seems to me equally unpersuasive. It is said, for instance, that an upward revaluation of gold would involve a
breach of faith with those who hold money other than gold.
I agree that this would be so if the change were to involve
ipso facto a change in the general purchasing power of
money; and for this reason I would oppose such a policy
unless safeguards were provided against such an event. But
if there is no such change directly consequential, I do not see
that the charge is valid. Ever since the ratification of the
IMF statutes, the holders of money other than gold have
held it subject to the risk of a change in price; and if they do

not suffer a loss in real values other than in terms of gold, I cannot believe that they are the subject of injustice.

Nor am I moved by the contention that the change proposed would involve economic benefit both to Russia and South Africa. It is clear that these regimes are not universally popular. But I cannot believe that if a change of the kind proposed were to be otherwise beneficial to the world at large, we should desist just because some areas with governments which are out of favor may enjoy side benefits. This seems to me a very unbalanced attitude.

Much more important seems to me to be the argument of the danger of inflation. I think this is a very real danger. If the banking authorities of the various areas, whose reserves were increased as a result of the change in the price of gold, were to make these increases the basis for an immediate extension of credit, then our last state would be worse than our first. If it were considered impossible to provide a safeguard against such developments, then I should be against this policy root and branch. But I should not have thought this difficulty to be altogether unsurmountable. The use which it has been proposed to make of the increase, the liquidation of reserves in media other than gold, whether or not desirable in other respects, would tend in this direction. And in any case, if the financial authorities of the world were to muster enough unity to change the price of gold in order to rectify a supposed unbalanced reserve position, it is surely legitimate to suppose that they could agree also upon self-denying ordinances as regards reserve ratios which would preclude inflationary developments.

For all these reasons, therefore, I find myself in a position in which I am not finally opposed to a policy of this sort. And I can conceive a situation in which, all other proposals being unacceptable and psychological collapse round the corner, I would even positively support it.

But having said this, I hasten at once to say that I should support it without enthusiasm. I should support it only as a *pis aller*—an expedient of last resort. I hope what I have said already will have shown the friends of this proposal that I am not among their uncomprehending opponents, yet I must confess that, from my point of view, it suffers from grave deficiencies.

In the first place, it must surely be regarded as a once-

for-all remedy—the mere idea of a repetition at intervals
would itself set in motion psychological impulses which
would go far to offset any present benefits. But a once-
for-all solution is not what is required by our analysis; or at
least, it is not what is required by the needs of liquidity—
the extinction of the gold-exchange standard, if it took
place, would perhaps fall into a different category. What
is required is a solution which provides for a gradual increase of reserves as production and trade expand. I
used to think that a rise in the price of gold would look
after this for some time. But there have recently been as-
surances, from those who ought to know, that for some
time at least the effect would be the reverse—the incentive
to prolong the life of the mines would lead immediately to
the exploitation of inferior resources. I do not think we
could count on private dishoarding to offset this for more
than a very short period.

But, quite apart from its inadequacy as a solution to the
prospective practical problem, I must confess that I find
further inadequacies in the general conception. I cannot
believe that the restoration of the gold standard old style,
even if it were politically practical—which I suspect it is
not—is the solution to the international monetary problem
as I enunciated it at the beginning of this paper. I do not
believe it is the solution to all the problems of lateral adjustment which are likely to arise in the modern world. Still less
do I believe that it begins to solve the problems of general
stabilization and common control of over-all purchasing
power, which it is so necessary to solve if the citizens of the
world are to tolerate the requirements of relative adjustment. I agree, as I have already admitted, that the record of
gold in the past compares very favorably with anything that
we have been able to do so far with managed currencies. But
in this, our modern age, we have eaten of the fruit of the
tree of knowledge in this respect. We know—or we think we
know—of better methods of managing our monetary fortunes than reliance on the vagaries of supply of and demand
for a precious metal, if only we could erect the appropriate
machinery and if only the politicians would allow it to work
according to plan. And although we may be naive in such
hopes, yet they are not likely to cease to influence action.
Thus, even when we have disabused ourselves of all the

misapprehensions and misconceptions which, in recent years, have befogged judgment of the gold standard and its potentialities, a great many of us are bound to regard it as at most a very second-best and to look elsewhere for superior solutions.

This being my frame of mind, you will not find it surprising that I am disposed to attend with considerable enthusiasm to the suggestions of those whose solutions to our problem lie in the direction of turning the IMF from a fund into a bank—a central bank for the free world, in which the national banks keep a substantial part of their reserves, and which, by way of open-market policy, has the power of easing or curbing the availability of purchasing power for the entire area over which it operates. This surely must be the ultimate solution to the problem from which we started, the problem of the absence of a common money and a common apparatus of control; and for me at any rate it is the yardstick by which I am disposed to judge other proposals for innovation and reform.

But while as an intellectual solution it is ideal, it is difficult to suppress doubts as to its immediate practicability. In a world of divided sovereignty, does sufficient confidence exist to make probable this not inconsiderable surrender of the right to independent initiative in the financial sphere? Does it exist even among the leading areas of what roughly can be called the West, which I confess is the world I am chiefly interested in?

But beyond this, is the Fund the appropriate institution to be charged with such momentous developments? Is its constitution such as to create the requisite confidence? It is at this point that I hark back to my regrets that the postwar monetary reconstruction did not start from the more restricted basis of the Tripartite Agreement, suitably enlarged, rather than from, as this would be, an all-embracing collection of all areas of the free world, great or small, strong or weak. I cannot help remembering what the weaker elements would have made of the quotas and the drawing rights at Bretton Woods had they not been resisted; and I confess that I was frankly appalled to discover that my good friend, Max Stamp, who has been one of the leading exponents of this idea of the transformation of the Fund into a bank, proposes to issue his newly created credits as bonuses, so to speak, to the so-called underdeveloped areas. This does not—repeat, not—mean that I am indifferent to the needs of such areas: I do not disapprove of properly administered loans or grants—I am a very great admirer of the work which is done by the Bank for International Reconstruction and Development and its subsidiaries. But it does mean that I do not believe that the best basis for the development of a good central banking tradition for the free world is an institution governed partly by those who are likely for generations ahead to be net borrowers, short and long, of the free world's capital accumulations.

It is for reasons of this sort that my hunch is that, for some time to come, we shall have to be content with solutions much less ambitious, much less logical and clear-cut, much more *ad hoc* and messy than the schemes I have just been discussing. I suspect that for the next few years at least we shall solve our problems of international liquidity in terms of some formalization of existing emergency arrangements between the leading central banks, and perhaps also in terms of the creation of supplementary reserve units linked in some way or other to gold, as suggested by Mr. Bernstein and other important authorities. I will not expatiate on the relative implications of alternative plans of this sort. I expect to learn much more about such matters in the course of our discussions. I will only say that if I were betting on the outcome of the present search at high levels for solutions to the liquidity problem, it would be on plans of this type that I would put my money.

But this is a judgment of practical probability. If I come back to the search for the ideal, I cannot but admit that I find this kind of contingency solution radically inferior to the more ambitious supranational banking solution; I am filled with regret that it should be the ceiling of ideas for practicable reform, and I ask myself, is it impossible to hope for some progress in the more ambitious direction? Is it impossible to hope that, in an area less miscellaneous than the area of the Fund, in an area more homogeneous in habits of mind and in economic conditions, there might be developments in the direction of a common money and a common control? Is it beyond reason to hope that some time there might be created something like a federal—or perhaps better said *confederal*—reserve system for the Atlantic Community as a whole?

But this brings us down to politics and issues far beyond the scope of this paper. I will therefore conclude only by expressing my strong conviction that, in the last analysis, all the issues that I have discussed, all the more technical issues that will be discussed, all ultimately depend on the question of whether the nations of the West have the spiritual resilience to transcend their present inappropriate political organization and form a supranational association more suited to the conditions of our age, or whether, weighed down by inertia and psychological atavisms inspired by recent painful experiences, they remain in a condition in which they are permanently vulnerable to the unfree powers and permanently incapable of giving the world at large a lead towards the superior conditions of which it would otherwise be capable.

*Milton Gilbert**

CHAPTER III

INTERNATIONAL LIQUIDITY:
THE PRESENT SITUATION

In analyzing the facts about international liquidity, we might hope to find the answers to three questions. First, we might hope that the facts would indicate with some precision just what the problems are. Secondly, the facts might indicate whether finding a solution to these problems is urgent or whether we can calmly talk about them year after year without doing anything. Thirdly, if we are a little more naïve, we may expect that the facts would point to the best solution, or at least to the available options. It is with these questions in mind that I intend to look at the present situation.

It is universally agreed that the chief difficulty with the present system is that—given the fact that gold is the basic reserve asset in the system—the amount of new gold available for monetary purposes each year does not allow for an adequate increase in global reserves. A second major difficulty is that the flow of dollars, which in an earlier period provided an acceptable reserve asset to supplement gold, cannot continue to play this role to the extent that it formerly did. First of all, it cannot do so because the United States would have to be continuously in deficit for foreign dollar holdings to grow, and nobody likes that—not even the United States. Furthermore, since dollars leaving the United States can be converted into gold, at least to some extent, there is a continuous drain on the U.S. gold stock,

---

* An expert's expert, Milton Gilbert has been the Economic Adviser of the Bank for International Settlements in Basle since 1960. Earlier (1951–60) he directed the economics staff of the OEEC in Paris and, still earlier (1941–51), he headed the National Income Division of the U.S. Department of Commerce. He is the author of *Currency Depreciation and Monetary Policy* and *An International Comparison of National Products and the Purchasing Power of Currencies* (with Irving B. Kravis).

bringing with it a threat to the stability of the whole system. Because of these difficulties, the Group of Ten has been considering the possibilities of "deliberate creation of reserves for global needs" and of "contingency planning" for some future time when a shortage of reserves might develop.

The first point I would make is that there is an element of fiction in this view, since we have already been dealing with a shortage of reserves for the past five or six years. The watershed year is really 1960, the year in which there was an eruption in the gold market, with the price for a brief time rising to $40 an ounce.

In Table III-1 I have compared the statistics for 1960–65 with the six years preceding. There are two significant differences between the periods. One is that in the latter period the annual growth of world reserves has been on a much higher level than before. The other difference is that, since 1960, the system has been managed to a much greater extent than before, and reserves have been created in completely new ways.

Table III-1
CHANGES IN TOTAL OFFICIAL RESERVES
(in millions of U.S. dollars and percentages)

Areas and years	Gold reserves Aggregate change ($)	Annual rate of increase (%)	Foreign exchange reserves Aggregate change ($)	Annual rate of increase (%)	Fund reserve positions Aggregate change ($)	Global reserves Aggregate change ($)	Annual rate of increase (%)
All countries							
1954–59	3,560	1.7	740	0.8	1,360	5,660	1.7
1960–65	4,045	1.7	6,350	5.7	2,125	12,520	3.3
Group of Ten and Switzerland							
1954–59	3,455	1.8	1,035	3.0	1,165	5,655	2.4
1960–65	2,595	1.3	3,900	8.2	1,615	8,110	2.9
Group of Ten excluding the United States and the United Kingdom							
1954–59	5,785	12.7	1,100	3.3	595	7,480	9.1
1960–65	8,285	9.6	2,600	6.0	3,075	13,960	9.9
Other developed countries							
1954–59	415	4.7	395	2.0	155	965	3.4
1960–65	1,530	11.2	1,110	4.8	330	2,970	7.6
Less-developed countries							
1954–59	−310	—	−690	—	40	−960	—
1960–65	−80	—	1,340	3.3	180	1,440	2.4

Let me recall some of the ways by which this has been done. In the IMF, for example, the General Arrangements to Borrow created a new pool of $6 billion, and it is indicative of certain attitudes toward gold that this IMF facility carried with it a gold guarantee—not the usual IMF gold value guarantee, but a gold guarantee. In addition, there has been an increase in quotas in the IMF which became effective in 1966 but which had been talked about for a few years before actually negotiated. This increase came before the normal five-year review of the Fund's position and carried with it—this is also indicative of a problem—what is called a "mitigation procedure" to ease the strain on the gold reserves of the reserve currency countries. There have also been very substantial drawings on the Fund—"technical" drawings and nontechnical or ordinary drawings. The former are a new phenomenon, arranged to provide currencies that debtors can use to repay drawings on the Fund now that the dollar cannot be used because the Fund's dollar holding is larger than the U.S. currency subscription.

Another kind of action has been the development of the U.S. "swap network" with the central banks of quite a few other countries, and this network has been increased several times since it was first set up. Then there has been the development of the technique of "Roosa bonds." These are bonds issued by the U.S. Treasury, but denominated in a foreign currency. There has also been the establishment of the Gold Pool to manage the gold market and prevent another speculative increase in the price, as in 1960. A more recent technique is Italy's deposit of $250 million worth of lire in the IMF in 1966, carrying with it a gold guarantee instead of the usual gold value guarantee.

Thus the authorities have been quite busy creating reserves. The very fact that these actions were taken obviously means that there was a need for reserves which was not being met by new gold or by new accumulation of dollars. Consequently it is rather meaningless to say that there has not been a shortage of reserves. One might say that, because of all the actions that were taken, there has been no shortage; or that there was a shortage and, therefore, some of these actions had to be taken. Either proposition is quite different, however, from the simple statement that there has been no shortage of reserves.

The point I want to stress is that, while "contingency planning" has always been spoken of with regard to possible reserve creation in the future, reserve creation has actually been going on for five years now. And it is quite clear that if none of these actions had been taken, the present exchange rate structure would not have survived.

Let us now turn to global reserves to see what the trends have been and how they have been affected by these actions I have been discussing. I avoid the term "international liquidity" because it is used in too many senses; by global reserves I mean simply the reserves of all central banks or monetary authorities taken together.

Traditionally, reserves were always international assets on the books of a monetary authority, more or less immediately available for intervention in the foreign exchange market to maintain the exchange parity of the currency. They were held in gold or convertible foreign exchange in liquid form, primarily dollars or sterling. However, as you may see from Table III-1, transactions with the IMF have become so important that figures for total reserves cannot have a clear meaning unless the gold-tranche positions in the IMF are included as part of reserves. Some countries include these IMF "reserve positions" in their reserve statistics and some do not, but in this table I have done so for all countries.

Looking at Table III-1, you will note that the increase in global reserves (i.e., in all three forms of reserves) for the period 1960–65 was more than double the increase for the period 1954–59—$12.5 billion compared to $5.7 billion. For all countries, the rate of increase rose from an average 1.7 per cent a year in the earlier period to an average 3.3 per cent a year in the later period. In part, this was because the reserve creation of the Fund had increased by 50 per cent and because gold reserves were about a half billion dollars higher in the second period. But the really big change was in the assets included in "foreign exchange reserves": in the first period, these increased by $740 million; in the second period, by $6,350 million. Quite a difference!

It may surprise some of you that the much larger increase in global reserves in the second period is accounted for mainly by the less-developed countries. In the earlier period such countries lost almost $1 billion of reserves; in the second period they gained $1.4 billion—a turn-around of $2.4 billion. In the 1950s these countries were suffering from the decline in raw material prices after the Korean war, and they did not recover from that unfortunate position for about a decade. But the more recent experience is quite encouraging; reserves have been going up at an average rate of 2.4 per cent a year, and it is this experience that has changed some attitudes about the participation of such countries in contingency planning that might be set in motion in the future.

What I have listed in the table as "other developed countries"—that is, developed countries not in the Group of Ten—also account for part of the sharp increase in global reserves. Their reserves in the second period went up $2 billion more than they did in the earlier period. It may be noted that of the world increase in global reserves in the second period, which amounted to about $7 billion, only $2.5 billion was acquired by the Group of Ten.

Another fact stands out in this table: the very sharp contrast between the Group of Ten as a whole, and the Ten excluding the United States and the United Kingdom. Rates of increase for the Group of Ten as a whole are under 3 per cent in both periods, as against over 9 per cent for the Ten excluding the United States and the United Kingdom. This explains why some members of the Group of Ten feel that reserves have been more than plentiful. They feel that they have been a little flooded with reserves, and even that they have suffered from some "imported inflation," as they call it. It is also obvious from the table that the United States and the United Kingdom, taken together, have lost reserves. In fact, this all happened to be a loss of reserves by the United States of just under $6 billion.

Now let us try to see how the actions described earlier, actions taken by monetary authorities to manage the system, have affected the growth of reserves.

In the earlier period, 1954–59, the accretion of reserves occurred in the normal way; countries acquired new gold or they held dollars, and there wasn't much by way of special influences on the growth of reserves. There were two special factors which I might mention. First was the liquidation of the European Payments Union, which had the effect of reducing foreign exchange reserves by $473 million. Secondly, there was a $500 million purchase of gold from the IMF by the United States that, in its effect, added $500 million to global reserves. Thus in their joint effect these two special factors just about offset each other.

In the later period, 1960–65, special transactions, whether or not we call them deliberate reserve creation, have been predominant. The IMF has been very much involved in this, but the figures do not accurately indicate the real impact of reserve creation through the Fund, because in the earlier period the increase in IMF positions of $1,360 million was all due to increased gold subscriptions, whereas in the later period the increase was primarily due to credit operations. There was also an additional U.S. purchase of gold from the Fund of $300 million.

The other special transactions which affected global reserves were concentrated in the foreign exchange component. In this period they consisted of the issuing of Roosa bonds and the creation of special central bank facilities, mainly in the form of swaps. These two kinds of special transactions account for $2 billion of the global foreign exchange reserve increase of $6,350 million.

Passing to the Group of Ten, we can use the same $2 billion figure, because all these special transactions were among the Group of Ten. That is to say, of the increase of $3.9 billion in the Ten's foreign exchange reserves, $2 billion, or a bit more than half, was by deliberate reserve creation, or by special transactions, however one may wish to look at it. If we exclude the United States and the United Kingdom from the Ten, the proportion of new foreign exchange reserves resulting from special transactions is considerably lower—$1 billion out of $2.6 billion.

Though the accumulation of foreign exchange reserves in the ordinary way—that is, in the form of dollars—increased by $1.6 billion in 1960–65, the entire increase actually took place in 1960. In that year, dollar holdings increased by $2,350 million; since 1960, foreign exchange reserves, omitting those arising from special transactions, have actually been declining, to the extent of $800 million. I might say, incidentally, that the decline has not been due to France, because France's dollar holdings were larger at the end of 1965 than at the end of 1960.

Apart from creating reserves, there have also been special transactions which have had the effect of reducing reserves. Without such transactions, the reserve increase would have been very much greater than that shown in the table. These transactions were undertaken at a time when there was a sort of *embarras de richesses* with respect to reserves, and they were of three sorts.

One technique was the prepayment of debts, a large part of it to the United States. This meant that the monetary authorities took funds out of reserves and paid debts before they were due. I have tried to calculate how much this amounted to on a net basis (because some debts prepaid, say, in 1961 might have been paid by 1965 anyway) and have arrived at a net figure of about $1.5 billion of reserves used to prepay debts in the period 1960–65.

A second technique for reducing reserves—or, rather, for reducing the growth of reserves—has been to facilitate commercial bank holding of foreign exchange balances; in other words, by special swap transactions, to shift foreign exchange balances from the central bank to the commercial banks. By the end of 1965 this technique had transferred to commercial banks $1.6 billion of foreign exchange that would otherwise have appeared in the global reserve figures.

The third factor which has had this effect has been the acquisition of foreign assets that are not counted as reserves. These appear in the balance sheet of the central bank, but not in reserves, and are sometimes called second line reserves. Generally, they are not as liquid as the first-line reserves. Such assets amount to $900 million.

In total, the special actions that have had the effect of reducing reserves amount to $4 billion. You can imagine what kind of reserve increase we would have had if, on top of the over-all increase of $12.5 billion, there had been another $4 billion; it would have been almost a runaway rate. Thus it is easy to understand why some countries stress the necessity of reaching a better equilibrium in the balance of payments rather than the need for more reserves.

What was the reason for all these special transactions? First of all, they were intended to provide reserves for the United States and the United Kingdom, the two main countries in deficit. Secondly, they were undertaken to convert some of the dollars acquired into another type of asset—or simply to reduce dollar holdings, because the central bank

did not want that amount of dollars in its reserves. And on
the part of the United States, a primary motive was to limit
the outflow of gold.

Let me go on to the facts about gold in Table III-1. You
will note that the increase in gold reserves for all countries
is $3.6 billion in the period 1954–59 and about $4 billion in
the period 1960–65. This is the increase in gold held by
countries in their reserves. It is not the same thing as the
total increase in gold in the system, because international
institutions also hold gold for monetary purposes—mainly
the International Monetary Fund and the Bank for International Settlements. Now in the first period the gold holdings
of international institutions increased by $389 million,
whereas in the second period countries took gold away from
international institutions to the extent of $940 million. Thus
total monetary gold stocks in the first period really went up
by $3.9 billion, or at an average annual rate of 1.7 per cent,
while in the second period they went up by $3.1 billion, or at
an average annual rate of 1.2 per cent.

The table shows that, in the second period, the amount of
gold gained by the Group of Ten (always including Switzerland, which actually makes it a group of eleven) was considerably less—nearly $1 billion less—than in the earlier pe-
riod. If the United Kingdom and the United States are
excluded, however, the Group gained more gold in the second period because, of course, the United States and the
United Kingdom lost gold. But it is worth noting that, even
in this smaller grouping, the increase in gold in relation to
the increase in reserves (including reserve positions in the
Fund) was actually less in the second period than in the
first.

Another fact I find interesting concerns the group labeled
"other developed countries," such as Spain, Austria, Den-
mark, Norway, and so on. The amount of gold they have
been putting into their reserves has gone up quite a lot—
from an increase of $415 million in 1954–59 to one of $1.5
billion in 1960–65. But even in this case, the amount of gold
going into reserves relative to the increase in reserves has
remained roughly the same. In other words, these countries
as a group have not shifted to any important extent from
other kinds of reserve assets toward gold, but have maintained about the same sort of reserve policy over-all.

Table III-2 is taken from the 1966 BIS report, but includes some preliminary figures for 1966. I will comment on it only briefly here, since it was discussed at length in the report. What the table shows is that the private demand for gold has about reached a point at which, when there are no Russian sales, as there were not in 1966, the market takes everything, leaving nothing for monetary purposes. Now, since countries other than the Group of Ten do continue to add some gold to their reserves, this means that when Russia does not sell, the Group of Ten is likely on balance to lose some gold.

Table III-2
SUPPLY AND USE OF GOLD

Year	Supply of gold			Net official purchases	Private demand		
	New production	Russian sales	Total		Reported industrial use (12 countries)	Other private absorption	Total
				(in millions of U.S. dollars)			
1953	845	75	920	455	.	.	465
1954	895	75	970	670	.	.	300
1955	940	75	1,015	665	.	.	350
1956	975	150	1,125	490	165	470	635
1957	1,015	260	1,275	690	195	390	585
1958	1,050	220	1,270	680	200	390	590
1959	1,125	300	1,425	750	220	455	675
1960	1,175	200	1,375	345	265	765	1,030
1961	1,215	300	1,515	600	285	630	915
1962	1,290	200	1,490	330	330	830	1,160
1963	1,355	550	1,905	840	325	740	1,065
1964	1,395	450	1,845	750	430	665	1,095
1965	1,430	550	1,980	400[a]	475	1,105	1,580
1966[b]	1,435	—	1,435	−55[c]	530	960	1,490

[a] Includes about $150 million of purchases by China.
[b] Preliminary estimates.
[c] Includes about $75 million of purchases by China.

Having looked at these facts, perhaps not so boring after all, what conclusions can we draw from them? First of all, I think we can say that the growth of global reserves has been quite adequate, tempering the remark by adding that this adequacy has depended upon the undertaking of a variety of special transactions. Without these transactions, the increase in reserves simply would not have been adequate. A second inescapable conclusion is that the problems in the system are entirely in the Group of Ten. Other countries have had no difficulty increasing their reserves without engaging in special transactions. Going back to my opening remarks, I think, then, that the facts do show us something about the nature of our problems.

Secondly, they show us that these problems not only are urgent, but that we have been dealing with them fairly continuously over the past five years.

As for my third reason for looking at the facts—the hope that they might point to a future solution—I am sorry to disappoint you; the kind of solution that is best depends not only on facts, but on one's vision of the world of the future. As it is sovereign states rather than I that must have this vision, I will conclude with that observation.

CHAPTER IV

THE RUEFF APPROACH

It is very generous to label my position "the Rueff approach" because, in large measure, my approach is also Professor Triffin's approach and Mr. Bernstein's approach. It was probably also the approach of the people who drafted the charter of the International Monetary Fund at Bretton Woods, and it was President Roosevelt's approach in 1934 when he changed the price of gold from $20 to $35 an ounce. So I don't think I deserve such an honor, but I take it as a duty to state as clearly as I can my views on gold and reform.

Generally speaking, my position is inspired by the conviction that we are not faced with a problem of lack of liquidity. We see in every country of the West, including Great Britain and now to some degree the United States, stabilization policies and "incomes policies"—evidence not of a lack but of an excess of liquidity. My friend Milton Gilbert has said that the Group of Ten is busy creating reserves; the operation, as he describes it, is "the deliberate creation of reserves for growing needs." But there is no growing need for reserves; there is a need for foreign exchange to pay for the American and British deficits—and nothing else.

It may be that in the future there will be some need for additional reserves. Then we will need to remember that the production of gold is not a fixed quantity. In 1928 I was a very young man with the League of Nations Secretariat, and I prepared a memorandum for the Gold Delegation—

* An economist of great distinction both in academic and official circles, Jacques Rueff is a member of the Académie Française, Chancellor of the Institut de France, an economic adviser to President de Gaulle, and a former vice governor of the Bank of France. He has served as a judge on the Court of Justice of the European Coal and Steel Community and, later, on the consolidated Court of the European Communities. Among his books are *The Age of Inflation* (1963) and *The Balance of Payments* (1967).

which, by the way, exactly like the Group of Ten, complained about the lack of liquidity. My memorandum showed that, up to 1914, the production of gold was seven times greater in periods of falling prices than in periods of rising prices. It is a truism, but also a most important statement, that gold production is influenced by the price mechanism. When commodity prices decline, this is equivalent to a relative increase in the price of gold, and when commodity prices rise, to a relative fall in the price of gold.

My main concern with the present situation is that it seems to *create* the balance-of-payments deficits of the key-currency countries. Here we have the old question of the hen and the egg: the creation of reserves is not just a result of the payments deficit of the United States and the United Kingdom; it is a *cause*.

It has been said that there surely has been no excess of aggregate demand in the United States. This is quite true; what has been wrong in the United States is the failure of aggregate demand to respond to a deficit in the balance of payments. To correct this situation is not simply a matter of returning to the gold standard, because the United States is still on the gold standard; any central bank can exchange its dollars for gold. But the gold standard is affected by an illness which has very serious symptoms. That illness is the gold-exchange standard. It is a kind of cancer, the result of which is, for example, that the very same day dollars are received in, say, France, they are returned to the money market in New York by cable and invested either in treasury bills or in bank deposits. I have seen this in practice; it is not just theory, but fact. Since 1960, this phenomenon has been dominant; and the fact that there has never been a contraction of aggregate demand corresponding to the deficit in the U.S. balance of payments explains why this deficit has continued—and will continue as long as there are countries ready to increase their dollar balances.

My friends in Washington agree that, because of the gold-exchange standard, there is no automatic contraction of credit in response to the payments deficit, but they say, "What money has not done, we can do by deliberate credit policy." I have told them, "Maybe you can do it, but there is no chance whatever that you *will* do it." In a year in which there has been a $3 billion deficit in the balance of payments, they could not reduce credit by such an amount. It may not be technically impossible, but it would certainly be politically impossible.

Thus the main question for me is not the price of gold; it is the question of the sensitivity of the level of aggregate demand to the balance-of-payments position. In my last little book on the balance of payments, which will shortly be published in the United States, I have cited about fifteen cases which are so precise that I think nobody can doubt the effectiveness of the adjustment mechanism when there is a link between internal demand and the balance of payments. Let us consider again the case of the United States, which, despite its payments deficit, has a surplus in its balance of trade. The trade surplus occurs because the United States is spending so much money abroad for aid, for military expenditure, and so on. It is because of its very generous contributions to the welfare of the world that the United States is always in trade surplus. When I was there in April, 1965, the Americans had just invented "self-restraint," and they proudly said, "You will see; it will restore the balance." I told them that it was fallacious to believe that the payments deficit could be cured by a reduction of expenditure abroad—military expenditure, aid expenditure—or, in other words, by "self-restraint." All the precedents show that this policy only reduces the surplus in the balance of trade and does not re-establish equilibrium. Since then, we have seen that the U.S. trade surplus has, in fact, become smaller, while the payments deficit has remained.

If I may, I would address to Dr. Emminger a request that the Group of Ten devote a part of its time to the study of past experiences in which the balance of payments has been brought back into equilibrium. I am sure that his group would find decisive cases which show clearly where the remedy is to be found.

To state my approach positively, I am in profound agreement with my dear friend Triffin about the diagnosis of the crisis. I think he has the great merit of having been one of the first to state the diagnosis. I did it in 1932—because I was much older than he—when the situation was the same. He had the great merit to do it later on.

As for the remedies, I do not believe that those put forth very logically by Mr. Triffin and by Mr. Bernstein will ever be applied. It is for that reason that I propose another approach. What I have in mind would need to be achieved through an international convention embracing the Group of Ten plus some other countries.

The countries would agree, first, not to increase, from a certain date onward, their reserve balances in dollars and sterling, this clause in no way interfering with the holding of working balances in these currencies. I put sterling and dollars together, though the case of sterling is somewhat different from that of the dollar. The fundamental need and objective is to create a situation in which the deficit country will lose what the surplus country gains.

In this connection I shall use an illustration which I have sometimes employed in the past. If I were to discover a tailor who would agree to return to me the amount of my bill on the very day I pay him, I would be much less cautious about ordering new suits, and my own balance of payments would be in deficit. That is the only secret of the deficit in the U.S. balance of payments: the United States has a deficit because the dollars it has used to settle the deficit have been returned to that country through the gold-exchange standard. The point is fundamental—all the rest is trivial.

To restore an effective payments system, something will have to be done about the existing dollar and sterling balances held as reserves. In the case of the dollar balances, you know the figures: Foreign countries at present have close to $14 billion in official dollar holdings, while the United States has about $13 billion in gold, almost $11 billion of which is immobilized as a cover for note circulation. The reserve requirement against notes could, of course, be changed, and I would not object to that. But if foreign central banks were to seek to convert any substantial part of their dollar holdings into gold, they would gravely disturb the situation and create the necessity for a U.S. embargo on gold.

I do not need to say that this is not simply a matter of French ill will. As you know, in 1965 the French demand accounted for only about half of the total gold outflow from the United States. After all, nobody can expect creditors to remain quiet when they see a deterioration of U.S. solvency. I do not mean a lack of wealth; the United States is by far the most powerful economy and by far the richest country in the world. This is a matter of monetary solvency, and you cannot expect central bankers who have dollars and who feel a responsibility toward their depositors to remain sitting idly, waiting silently for the day when their dollar holdings may no longer be convertible into gold.

Thus, if you want to restore an effective system of payments, you must get rid of the great part of the dollar and sterling balances. So the second point of the convention would be to increase simultaneously, and in the same proportion, the price at which central banks purchase and sell gold. The amount of the increase would be decided by common agreement, but one can foresee that, since the price level in the United States has doubled since 1934—when the gold price was fixed at its present level by President Roosevelt—the new gold price should be approximately doubled. Because of the great improvement since 1934 in techniques for extracting gold, a smaller increase might be acceptable, provided the price were set at a proper level in relation to the cost of production.

As a third point, the United States and Great Britain would agree to devote a part of the increase in the nominal value of their respective gold stocks to the immediate repayment in gold of the dollar and sterling balances in the hands of central banks. I consider that the greater part of the dollar balances ought in this way to be repaid. The situation regarding the sterling balances is different, because much of the sterling is in the hands of Commonwealth countries, with which there are reliable "gentlemen's agreements"; therefore, I would not insist that all of the sterling balances be repaid, but would leave to the British government the question of deciding the proper amount.

If the price of gold were approximately doubled, the official dollar balances could be paid off in gold without affecting the dollar value of the remaining U.S. gold holdings. The $13 billion of U.S. gold would be worth $26 billion at the new price and, of this, the United States could use about half to repay the central banks, while retaining the same cash position in terms of dollars. Thus the change in the gold price would involve no risk of deflation or inflation for the United States.

For Britain, the situation would be quite different. Britain has about $2 billion in gold. If the gold price were doubled, that would mean $4 billion. This would be only enough to repay a third of the $12 billion in outstanding sterling balances, even if the entire British gold stock were used for that purpose. But these $12 billion in sterling balances, as I said before, are really profoundly different in character from the dollar balances, and I repeat that it should be for the British government to decide what it thinks necessary to repay.

Nevertheless, if we are to re-establish an efficient international monetary system, it is essential that the British government be in a position to repay those sterling balances that it deems necessary to repay; and this brings me to the fourth point in the convention. Apart from the key-currency countries, there would be important countries which have gold and which have no balances to repay. If the price of gold were doubled, the nominal value of their gold stocks would be correspondingly increased. Therefore, I propose that these countries offer Britain a twenty- or twenty-five-year loan equal to the amount of the sterling balances which were not already consolidated *de jure* or *de facto*, thus enabling the British government to repay these balances. This is not an extraordinary proposal; between the two wars, we often did things of this kind. When I was at the Treasury in France, we offered large loans to Great Britain, and, in the reverse direction, Britain on various occasions made available important resources to us. This is in the best tradition of treasury operations, and I am convinced that the credit of Britain is such that there would be no difficulty whatever in working out such a loan.

The loan, however, would absorb only a part of the nominal surplus resulting from the increase in the price of gold. I propose that some of the remaining surplus be devoted, by common agreement, to aid to developing countries in the form of loans. The loans could be made through existing institutions, or by using the surplus to provide capital for a new institution, or by simple transfer to the developing countries. This is a matter which should be discussed in common by those directly concerned.

Finally, the remaining surplus ought to be devoted, again by common agreement, to the repayment of debts—especially debts to central banks.

If all these things were done, international settlement in gold could be restored without any danger of insolvency among the deficit countries. To be realistic, however, we must concede that such a plan will not be put into operation so long as it goes against the grain of public opinion in the United States. It is very important, therefore, to meet this objection.

As I see it from the outside, public opinion in the United States is inclined to object to a change in the price of gold for a number of distinct reasons. It has been argued that such a step would be incompatible with monetary stability; that it would be reactionary, retrograde, inequitable; that it would be contrary to American and British interests; that it would be unduly favorable to gold-producing countries such as South Africa and the Soviet Union; and finally—the main argument—that it would be an outrage to the honor of the United States. I learned of this last argument at a meeting in New York, when my old friend Bill Martin said, "After all, and above everything, it is a matter of the honor of the United States." If this were true, I really would never propose a plan of this kind. I have not forgotten our debts to the United States and Great Britain—not just in the financial meaning of the word, but in the political and existential meaning—and I would not make a proposal injurious to the United States. Therefore, I will try to meet these objections.

First, there is the argument that an increase in the price of gold would be dangerous to monetary stability. Is it really possible to consider as reasonable a policy which would maintain one price alone—the price of gold—at the level chosen in 1934 by President Roosevelt, when the commodity price level in the United States was only half as high as it is now? Imagine what you would think of such a policy if it were applied to wheat or steel. The need for gold is approximately proportional to the general level of prices. Is it reasonable to maintain artificially the value of the existing gold stock and of the yearly production of gold at half of what it would be if gold were restored to its normal place in the hierarchy of prices? To maintain the price of gold at its 1934 level is to impose a very dangerous handicap on the international monetary system through an artificial limitation on the value of existing stocks of gold and of current production.

It is true that, under normal conditions, absence of change in the price of the monetary standard is the basis of the mechanism through which it can maintain the stability of the commodity price level over long periods. Thus in 1914 the index of prices in the United States was approximately the same as in 1820, despite an immense increase in production and despite the temporary upheaval of the Civil War. But to maintain the stability of the commodity price level, the monetary mechanism must operate continuously. Twice in the past half century, it has ceased to function—during World War I, when the U.S. price level increased by 50 per cent, and during World War II, when the price level more than doubled. After such a change, there are only two choices for the country wishing to restore freedom of international payments—either a reduction of commodity prices, restoring them to the level of the monetary parity, or an increase in the price of gold to a level corresponding to the change in the general level of prices. The first method—a reduction in the price level—is the remedy which Britain tried to apply in 1925. The result was more than a million unemployed, and the policy finally had to be abandoned. But at that time the problem was only an adjustment of 10 per cent. Imagine the disaster which would result in the United States from a policy aiming at a 50 per cent reduction in the price level! That is why I argue that the price of gold should be changed. Such a change would be once and for all, provided there is no new world war and provided there is no re-establishment of the gold-exchange standard regime. Contrary to the view that a change in the price of gold would be dangerous to monetary stability, the situation is just the reverse: a change in the price of gold is necessary for the achievement and maintenance of monetary stability.

Second, let us consider the argument that a change in the price of gold would be reactionary and retrograde. Those who oppose the suppression of the gold-exchange standard see in this step a return to the monetary system of our grandfathers. But this is a great mistake. It is not a question of re-establishing the gold standard, because the gold standard exists now, as I have said. President Roosevelt did not destroy, but re-established, the gold standard through an increase in the price of gold. Similarly, a change in the price of gold now would not be a return to the past, but a correction of a mistake which was sowing the seeds of a great world depression.

Third, a word about the argument that a change in the price of gold would be inequitable. The maintenance of the gold price at its 1934 level offers to anybody producing a certain weight of wheat or steel, or any product whose price has doubled since 1934, a weight of gold which is double what he would have received then in exchange for his product. Is it fair, equitable, or just, when gold is scarce and when the world is trying to limit the demand for gold, to offer such an inducement to obtain gold for what one produces?

Fourth, we come to the argument that a change in the price of gold would be contrary to American interests. The last time I was in the United States, I paid a visit to an important American senator, who said to me, "I know very well what the policy of your country is; you want to take all our gold; then you will double the price and make an enormous profit at our expense." I told him, "My dear friend, it is just the reverse. Our advice is to double the price of gold while you still have it, and to give us only half the amount we are entitled to ask you against our dollar balance." It is not a French position I am defending; it is a position in the interest of the whole world, for the sole purpose of reestablishing an effective international monetary system.

Fifth, let us take a look at the argument that a change in the price of gold would be unduly favorable to certain gold-producing countries, such as Russia and South Africa. Consider first the case of Russia. All the information I have appears to show that the cost of producing gold in Russia is very high and that Russia would prefer to pay for its imports, not in gold, but in goods. But suppose that a change in the price of gold were to make it easier for Russia to include gold among its exports. What is so bad about selling what we produce in exchange for Russian gold as well as for Russian wheat, steel, and coal? With respect to South Africa, the people who are opposed to an increase in the price of gold because they do not want to aid South African production are the same people who fear that the present system is leading to deflation. But you cannot have an increase in gold production and refuse to pay the price.

We come finally to the last point—the argument of my friend Bill Martin that changing the price of gold would impair the honor of the United States. But why? The dollar

balances have no gold clause attached to them. No court in
the world—and I have been a judge for ten years on the
Court of the European Community—has ever ruled that the
gold clause would apply where it has not been expressly
stipulated. To behave as if a gold clause existed where it
does not exist is to make a free gift to the holders of dollar
balances at the expense of the debtor country, the United
States. These holders cannot claim to have a moral, implicit
right to a gold clause, as is proved by the fact that some of
them have expressly obtained a gold guarantee. One must
not confuse the two kinds of claims; either there is a gold
clause or there is not. If there is not, there is no moral right
to repayment at a fixed value in gold.

The honor of a debtor nation lies in its ability to continue
repaying its debts. I am sorry to say that, in the present
circumstances, nobody can imagine that the United States,
in the absence of a new policy, will be able to repay the
dollar balances unless it issues a fully inconvertible guarantee. Would it be less of a reflection on the honor of the
United States to change the status of the dollar and to
repay in a currency inconvertible into gold? It would seem
to me much more honorable to apply an article which has
been written into the charter of the International Monetary
Fund—an article designed for exactly the situation in which
we are today.

In conclusion, I am absolutely convinced that the price of
gold will be changed, because there is no other practical
solution which is economically sound and morally acceptable
that has a chance, politically, of being accepted. The only
question which is fundamental is—when? If the change is
made à *froid*, before a crisis, the world will have been saved
the horror of a new depression. If it is not, then what shall
we have? Import quotas in the United States, exchange
control, and finally, I am sorry to say, an embargo on gold.
This will be a disastrous conclusion to all that has been
accomplished in the past ten years and to all the efforts
which are now being made toward the liberalization of
trade. It will be an immense setback in civilization that
must be avoided at any cost; and that is the reason we must
find somewhere enough statesmanship so that an effective
and practical remedy will be applied before it is too late.

CHAPTER V

THE TRIFFIN APPROACH

It is tempting for me to begin by commenting on the large amount of common ground which I find with Monsieur Rueff's diagnosis and with Dr. Bernstein's prescription, but this is not the appropriate time to do that and, instead, I shall take as my point of departure the eloquent opening address of Lord Robbins. At the outset, I must say that I am absolutely delighted with the way in which Lord Robbins has stated the problem and with his conclusions. In contrast to Mr. Giscard d'Estaing, I am strongly tempted to say *"oui"* without any *"mais"*—"yes" without any "but." This may surprise some of you; so I would like to explain why I do not really find any difference at all between what Lord Robbins has said and my own view of the problem.

In a world where countries have become more and more interdependent, he stressed the enormous gap between the supranational nature of the problem with which we must deal and the multiplicity of national currencies, coupled with nationally determined policies which are often internationally incompatible. Yet it is clearly impossible to change overnight these tribal or national systems with which we have been living into a supranational system in which countries are called upon to surrender their precious sovereignty. This is a problem we can only solve gradually— through international, not supranational, decisions. What I

* Robert Triffin achieved early fame as the head of numerous monetary and central banking missions to Latin American and other countries. He has held high staff positions at the Federal Reserve Board and the International Monetary Fund, and, as special adviser to the Economic Cooperation Administration, he played a leading role in the creation of the European Payments Union. Since 1951 he has been professor of economics at Yale, where he has held the Pelatiah Perit chair since 1958. His books include *Monopolistic Competition and General Equilibrium Theory* (for which he received the coveted Wells Prize at Harvard), *Europe and the Money Muddle*, *Gold and the Dollar Crisis*, and *The World Money Maze*.

would insist upon, however, is that in doing this we should not forget that the problem itself is not a national one: it is an international problem.

As was stressed by the famous group directed by Professor Machlup, the three basic problems confronting us are: First, what is the proper use of reserves? Second, what is the proper amount and rate of growth of reserves, given the purposes which we have defined in answering the first question? And third—to my mind the most urgent consideration at the moment—what is the proper composition of reserves? How can we live with several different types of reserve assets which countries can shift from one to another at any moment of time? This seems to me the most critical problem to be solved, and I regret that full attention has not been given to it in the official discussions—for perfectly understandable reasons, of course, in view of the disturbances which an open discussion might create in the market.

What are the solutions to these problems? Here we need, I think, to consider four questions. The first question to ask is: Who lends? There can be only one answer to that. Only those who save can lend; only the countries in balance-of-payments surplus can really lend to the others. The second question is: Who borrows? Again, there is only one answer. The countries in surplus can lend only to the countries in deficit. The third question is, how much, and here I would agree very much with the conclusions, as well as the way they have been stated, of Dr. Emminger in his last report.[1] Finally, the fourth question is: For what purpose? On this matter, the essential consideration, it seems to me, is that the lending should be for commonly agreed purposes; and, in this connection, I am afraid that people whose major objection to the Triffin Plan is the surrender of sovereignty which its adoption would involve forget that in the present system there is far more total, blind surrender of sovereignty than any required in my proposals. As the French have so clearly understood, anyone who accumulates fidu-

---

[1] Deliberate reserve creation should be geared to *long-term* trends in *global* needs for reserves rather than to cyclical trends or national balance-of-payments deficits. The amounts to be created should be such as to promote orderly growth, avoiding world-wide inflationary as well as deflationary pressures on the general stability of the system. (*Report to Ministers and Governors by the Group of Deputies*, July 7, 1966, p. 18, paragraph 98.)

ciary reserves in the form of the national currency of another country is lending to that country—and lending, moreover, without any control over the purposes for which the funds are used. In actual fact, the French object to the surrender of their sovereignty to the New York banks or to the U.S. Treasury, to help finance through the Bank of France what they rightly or wrongly regard as an excessive amount of private direct investment by the United States and the "take-over," to use their word, of French property, of French firms; or they may object similarly to financing the escalation of the war in Vietnam. I think that these are problems which can no longer be escaped and which must be faced very frankly, even bluntly, if we are to make any progress.

I agree with Lord Robbins that the ideal solution to this problem is not for tomorrow; it has never been for tomorrow. This world is dominated by one iron law, I would say, and that is the law of evolution. Unfortunately, this law is commonly ignored both by the conservatives on the right and by the radicals on the left. The conservatives live under the illusion that they can stop evolution, or even reverse it, returning for instance to a gold standard which is described in terms that do not even accord with any historical precedent—the gold standard simply never existed as it is described today.[2] It would, of course, be very comfortable for men to adhere to some sort of automatic system through which they could escape the responsibility for managing their own affairs. I am very much convinced, however, that this is a will-o'-the-wisp, and that neither God nor gold will manage man's affairs for him.

The radicals, at the other extreme, live under another illusion: that they can start from scratch and ignore the systems and institutions inherited from the past, of which they are in part prisoners. If we understand evolution, I think we are aware that things will change, and that we should change them in time to avoid crises; because many of the crises in the past, whether political or economic, have come from too long delays in adjusting institutions to changing realities. I think, for example, that the real cul-

---

[2] See my Princeton study on *The Evolution of the International Monetary System* ("Studies in International Finance," No. 12; Princeton: International Finance Section, Princeton University, 1964).

prits of the Russian revolution or of the Nazi revolution were not Lenin or Hitler, but the people who preceded them, who did not face the problems of their time.

In this connection I would like to add one point to Lord Robbins' conclusions, a point with which I think he will not disagree. I agree with him that we will have to live for some time with expedients, that we will not reach an ideal solution tomorrow. But realizing that, and accepting fully the philosophy which he has described, I still think it is very important to try to design these expedients in such a way that they will not be blind alleys, but rather will facilitate evolution in the direction which he himself has traced.

To descend from these academic heights to the current negotiations, I would stress once again a factor which we tend to forget—particularly we economists. I refer here to a special phenomenon inherent in the negotiating process itself. I am afraid that when diplomats enter the negotiating room, they tend very quickly to forget all that unites them—even though it be 90 per cent of the issues—and to concentrate their attention and their fire on the minor issues in which they feel, rightly or very often wrongly, that their national interests may diverge. They commence negotiations with totally incompatible, so-called negotiating or even bluffing positions, each trying to pull the whole blanket toward himself. And once the discussions have been established on that basis, they begin the process of bargaining and haggling, trying to reconcile these incompatible viewpoints into some form of limping compromise. The basic issues on which they may completely agree are forgotten.

I would like to elaborate, but I will simply say there that, to a discouraging degree, this has been the experience in the process of negotiation in the Group of Ten. What has happened is that we have gradually trapped ourselves into a situation in which we are now condemned, I think, to proceed on the basis of the CRU plan, which was originally and explicitly designed to freeze out the underdeveloped countries, for fear that they would impart an inflationary tendency to the system. Actually, far from having frozen them out, we have gradually had to make room for a 25 or 35 per cent participation; and we have further whetted their appetite by brandishing the possibility of some kind of manna from Heaven which initially they would have been denied.

But now, at this stage, it is too late to turn back, and the outcome of the negotiations will be influenced very much more by this haggling process than by the basic interests originally at stake.

We economists are far too prone these days to prostitute our own science by acting, not as economic advisers, but as psychoanalysts, trying to guess what Monsieur Debré may accept, or yesterday Giscard d'Estaing, or tomorrow somebody else. I think this is a game we should leave to the politicians; in any case, it certainly should not dominate our advice.

But while unwilling to make any kind of short-run prediction, I am more willing to be a bold prophet for the longer-term future. It is safer to make long-run prophecies than short-run forecasts, because one can depend on some basic historical trends which to my mind are completely uncontroversial. In that context, I think there have been two very clear trends in relation to the problem we are discussing: In the national monetary field, we have witnessed, over the years, commodity money gradually being displaced by fiduciary money, at first in the form of multiple fiduciary money issued by a multiplicity of institutions without any centralized control. In the next stage, fiduciary money completely replaced commodity money, but it had to be centralized somehow under the national monetary authorities. This happened everywhere in the world on a national basis; it has already started happening in the international monetary system as well. International commodity reserves, the gold and silver of former days, are gradually being displaced by multiple fiduciary reserves—reserve assets such as dollars and sterling and, to a minor extent, some other currencies.

Today we can see the third phase—a gradual tendency toward the establishment of centralized reserves in the form of reserve positions in the IMF, as noted by Milton Gilbert. In 1937, gold (commodity money) made up about 91 per cent of world monetary reserves. For countries other than the reserve-currency countries themselves (i.e., the United States and the United Kingdom) this figure had dropped to 49 per cent in mid-1966. And of the total held by these countries in fiduciary reserves, over one-fifth (22 per cent) consisted of reserve positions in the Fund.

This kind of development is clearly one that can be fitted into a much broader framework. But it is quite possible that, in the years immediately ahead, lack of agreement among the Group of Ten, or in other negotiations, may very well slow down, or even temporarily reverse, the long historical process I have described—possibly at the cost of a tragic crisis. I would rather believe, however, that the situation will not be quite so catastrophic as that. If we fail to reach agreement on long-range solutions, we may do what we did in the late 1940s and early 1950s: we may escape disaster through various kinds of expedients, with more and more bilateral swap arrangements between central banks, just as we had many bilateral payments agreements in the late 1940s. Later, however, those bilateral agreements were merged into multilateral agreements through the European Payments Union, which in the end led to a return to convertibility of all the major currencies. In the same fashion, we may take the same kind of devious road in the years just ahead, building on various sorts of expedients that people are willing to accept.

I will therefore conclude that, in the long run, there is hardly room for doubt that we will move through a process which may be faster or slower, more orderly or less orderly, in the direction of a centralization of world reserves. And I do indeed believe that this kind of trend can be fitted into a much broader view of man's faith—the kind of vision of the evolution of the world which has been outlined by such men as Teilhard de Chardin and, more recently, Jean Charon. Throughout his history, man has been groping toward a greater control over his own fate; and the success of this groping in a more and more international world involves a gradual adaptation of his tribal institutions to the realities of growing interdependence.

*Edward M. Bernstein**

CHAPTER VI

THE BERNSTEIN APPROACH

GOLD AND THE INTERNATIONAL MONETARY SYSTEM

There is a great deal of wishful thinking about gold. Some enthusiasts think that gold was especially designed to be the basis for an ideal monetary system. In fact, the gold standard was developed late in modern history, it lasted briefly in its classical form, and it has survived only because it has evolved to meet the practical needs of the world economy. Even in the period of its greatest prestige, prior to World War I, the old-fashioned gold standard was not a satisfactory basis for the monetary system by the criteria of today.

The best test of whether the gold standard provided a satisfactory monetary system is the degree of price stability that it achieved. Obviously, there was an exaggerated instability of prices from 1914 to 1934 because of the wartime inflation and postwar deflation. But as Chart VI-1 shows, even from 1851 to 1914, when there were only a few major wars in Europe, the price level rose and fell considerably for long periods—rising from 1851 to 1873, falling from 1873 to 1896, and rising again from 1896 to 1914. In these long waves, the average annual rise or fall of prices was about 2 per cent, so that the cumulative price change was 50 per cent or more in the course of 20 or 25 years. The cause of the alternate inflation and deflation was the very uneven rate of growth of the monetary gold stock. It is inevitable that gold production, depending on the fortuitous discovery of mines and on advances in mineral technology, should be either too much or too little for the world's monetary needs.

* Long noted as one of the leading American experts in international finance, Dr. Bernstein served for many years as a top U.S. Treasury official, as a key figure at the Bretton Woods conference of 1944, and as the first director of research and statistics at the International Monetary Fund. He is founder and president of EMB (Ltd.), a firm of research economists in Washington, D.C.

Chart VI-1

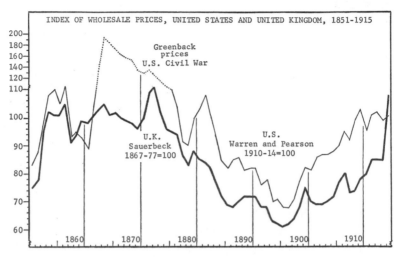

INDEX OF WHOLESALE PRICES, UNITED STATES AND UNITED KINGDOM, 1851-1915

PRODUCTION OF GOLD, QUINQUENNIEL PERIODS, 1841–1915
(Thousands of fine ounces annually)

1841–45	1,267	1866–70	6,243	1891–95	7,882
1846–50	2,255	1871–75	5,405	1896–00	12,447
1851–55	6,187	1876–80	5,340	1901–05	15,607
1856–60	6,361	1881–85	4,940	1906–10	20,971
1861–65	5,975	1886–90	5,461	1911–15	22,259

The view that the gold standard provided the discipline necessary for monetary stability is an illusion. In ordinary times, the rigid tie between the money supply and gold reserves resulted in recurring depressions and occasionally in monetary crises. In periods of emergency, and particularly in time of war, no country permitted the increase in its money supply to be restrained by the link to gold. Thus, every great war brought an enormous inflation, despite the gold standard. And what is worse, the gold mystique imposed a destructive deflation as the aftermath of a return to the traditional gold standard. The fact is that the classical gold standard did not provide monetary stability, even under the most favorable conditions, because it could not.

Some of the foremost supporters of the gold standard recognized that gold production could not provide the right amount of monetary gold to maintain a stable price trend. They proposed to deal with this problem by regulating either the demand for gold or the supply of gold. In 1919, R. G. Hawtrey wrote: "If we are going to adhere to the gold standard in the future, it is most desirable that the absorption of gold for currency purposes should everywhere be kept in control . . . We want so to regulate the demand for gold that the value . . . does not vary substantially."[1] Gustav Cassel gave strong support to this view.[2]

The principle that the value of gold must be managed was widely accepted after World War I. In April, 1922, the Genoa Conference recommended that each country should manage its monetary system to maintain the gold parity of its currency, while the central banks should act together to stabilize the value of gold. In fact, the Genoa Conference recommended that central bank co-operation be formalized through an international convention for "economizing the use of gold by maintaining reserves in the form of foreign balances, such, for example, as the gold-exchange standard, or an international clearing system."[3]

There were other proposals in the 1920s for stabilizing the long-run value of gold through regulations of the supply. Professor R. A. Lehfeldt of the University of the Witwatersrand suggested that the leading nations form a syndicate to acquire the gold mines and operate them to assure an appropriate supply of gold. "The output would have to be placed under the control of some authority that could take the long view, and act in the interest of the world, instead of that of the shareholders in the mines."[4] Even Lehfeldt admitted, however, that such proposals to control gold production "are too much in the clouds."[5]

The distinction between managing the demand for gold and managing the supply of gold is an analytical device. The relevant supply and demand are not for gold, but for monetary reserves. Economizing on the demand for gold means

---

[1] R. G. Hawtrey, *Monetary Reconstruction* (London: Longmans, Green and Co., 1923), pp. 48, 50–54.

[2] Gustav Cassel, *Money and Foreign Exchange after 1914* (London: Constable & Co., 1922), p. 263.

[3] Resolution 9 of the Genoa Conference. The text of the Genoa resolutions is reproduced in the Hearings of the U.S. Congress on the Strong Bill, Stabilization Hearings, 1927, pp. 957–58.

[4] R. A. Lehfeldt, *Restoration of the World's Currencies* (London: P. S. King & Son, Ltd., 1923), pp. 56–60.

[5] R. A. Lehfeldt, *Money* (London: Oxford University Press, 1926), p. 108.

holding reserve assets other than gold; and this requires a
supply of other reserve assets that are equivalent to gold.
The only practical distinction between gold and foreign exchange as monetary reserves is that gold is a final reserve
asset while foreign exchange is not. That is why so much
consideration has been given to creating a reserve asset
similar to foreign exchange but having the characteristic of
gold as a final reserve asset. In 1933, Keynes proposed that
an international monetary authority be established to issue
gold notes to a maximum of $5 billion, which would be
allocated among participating countries in exchange for an
equal amount of their gold bonds bearing a low rate of
interest.[6] The Reserve Unit proposal obviously belongs to
this family of plans for regulating the supply of reserves.

There is still another way of regulating the supply of
gold, and that is through a change in its price. In the 1930s,
the gold reserves of the world were increased by 70 per cent,
in monetary terms, through the successive devaluations of
all the leading currencies—sterling, then the dollar, and
finally the currencies of the gold bloc (France, Belgium,
the Netherlands, and Switzerland). This was not a concerted move to raise the price of gold. Actually, devaluation
was resisted by all countries, and particularly by the gold
bloc, until they were overwhelmed by the deflation and
depression—considerably intensified within the gold bloc by
the prior depreciation of sterling and the dollar.

Some economists see a dangerous parallel between the
reserve situation today and that of the 1920s, and they
propose to increase the present level of reserves, stimulate
future gold production, and raise the proportion of gold in
total reserves through a simultaneous and uniform increase
of 50 to 100 per cent in the price of gold in terms of all
currencies. There are strong objections to such a step. It
would result in a sudden and enormous increase in total
monetary reserves. It would arbitrarily redistribute the
world's monetary reserves on the basis of the present composition of a country's reserves—that is, in favor of those
that hold gold rather than dollars or sterling as reserves. A
change in the price of gold would be a breach of faith by the
United States and the United Kingdom with countries that

[6] J. M. Keynes, *The Means to Prosperity* (New York: Harcourt,
Brace and Co., 1933), pp. 28–30.

hold their currencies as reserves. It would give prizes to
hoarders and speculators, and it would reward with windfall profits those that regard gold as a speculative investment rather than as a monetary reserve.

Such a measure would mean the destruction of the gold
standard. One can justify the successive devaluations of the
1930s as brought on by *force majeure* and submitted to
unwillingly by all of the great industrial countries. One
could not justify a concerted reduction in the gold parity of
all currencies in a period of unmatched prosperity. The
supporters of a higher price of gold have presented elaborate proposals for making sure that the marking up of the
gold reserves of the United States and the United Kingdom
would be used to liquidate foreign dollar and sterling holdings. These proposals would merely assure an even greater
deficiency of reserves in these two countries. For the industrial countries of continental Europe, a rise in the price of
gold would mark up their gold reserves by $9.5 billion (50
per cent) or $19 billion (100 per cent). Perhaps in time the
sudden increase in gold reserves would be better distributed
among all countries. That would require a vast inflation in
the European countries that would have acquired large excess reserves.

The long-run justification of a higher price of gold must
be that it would permit the growth of gold reserves at an
appropriate rate. This seems to be an unattainable objective
in view of the uncertain effect of a higher price of gold on
private hoarding and dishoarding. What assurance is there
that the new price of gold would call forth neither substantially more nor substantially less gold production (after
allowing for changes in hoards) than is needed for an appropriate growth of monetary reserves? If the growth of
monetary reserves should prove to be too much or too little,
would the price of gold be changed repeatedly until just the
right amount of gold is available for the growth of monetary reserves? And if the price of gold can be raised and
lowered as a means of regulating the growth of reserves,
what is the significance of defining currencies in terms of
gold?

Some advocates of a higher price of gold hope that this
will make it possible to dispense with monetary management. On the contrary, it would increase the need for mone-

tary management by introducing a novel and disturbing element into the monetary system. It is impractical and unnecessary to regulate the growth of monetary reserves through changes in the price of gold. In my opinion, if there were no other means of dealing with the reserve problem except through a rise in the price of gold, some countries, and perhaps many, would decide to give up the gold standard and refuse to buy and sell gold at a fixed price. They would justly conclude that they could manage their monetary affairs in a better, if not fully satisfactory, way in a system of fluctuating exchange rates freed from a changing price of gold.

FOREIGN EXCHANGE AS MONETARY RESERVES

Since the end of the war, there have been far-reaching changes in the role of gold in monetary reserves. From the beginning of 1950 to the end of 1966, the monetary gold stock of the world, excluding the Communist bloc but including the International Monetary Fund and other international institutions, has grown at an average annual rate of less than 1.4 per cent. Despite this, the total monetary reserves of all countries, excluding the Communist bloc, increased at an average annual rate of 2.7 per cent. While total monetary reserves were growing at this moderate rate, world trade grew at an average annual rate of 7.5 per cent. At the same time, there was a radical redistribution of reserves from the United States to the industrial countries of Europe and the rest of the world. Both the growth of reserves and the redistribution of reserves were essential for the expansion of world trade and the restoration of currency convertibility. The growth of reserves in other forms made good the deficient growth of gold reserves and made it possible for world trade and payments to expand.

As Chart VI-2 shows, the growth of total reserves of all countries since the beginning of 1950 has been mainly in foreign exchange and primarily in the form of dollars. In this period of seventeen years, the gold reserves of all countries outside the Communist bloc (but excluding the IMF and other international institutions) increased by about $7.5 billion. On the other hand, their foreign exchange reserves increased by $12.8 billion, of which nearly $11 billion was in dollars, and their net creditor claims on the IMF increased by over \$4.6 billion. As such claims on the IMF (the gold tranche) can be drawn with assurance, they have the attribute of reserves. Most of these net creditor claims originated in gold subscriptions to the IMF, and the rest are the result of drawings of the currencies of surplus countries by other members.

Chart VI-2

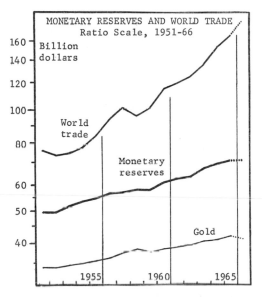

The redistribution of monetary reserves that has taken place since 1950 is evident from the change in the relative proportion of reserves held by the United States and by the industrial countries of continental Europe. At the beginning of 1950, the United States held 73.4 per cent of the gold reserves and 57.2 per cent of the total reserves of all countries outside the Communist bloc. The industrial countries of continental Europe held 10.2 per cent of the gold reserves and 11.1 per cent of the total reserves of all countries. At the end of 1966, the United States held about 32.4 per cent of the gold reserves and about 20.9 per cent of the total reserves of all countries. The industrial countries of continental Europe held about 46.1 per cent of the gold reserves and 43.0 per cent of the total reserves of all countries.

The growth of reserves and the redistribution of reserves since 1950 were the result of the large and prolonged deficit in the U.S. balance of payments. Whatever criticism may be made of the U.S. payments policy, it cannot be denied that the U.S. deficits were indispensable to the growth of monetary reserves and to a highly desirable redistribution of reserves. On the other hand, the growth of foreign exchange reserves has changed the structure of the reserve system. At the beginning of 1950, gold constituted 73.5 per cent of total reserves. At the end of 1966, gold constituted about 58 per cent of total reserves, the rest consisting of dollars, sterling and other foreign exchange, and net creditor claims on the IMF. These trends are shown in Chart VI-3.

Chart VI-3

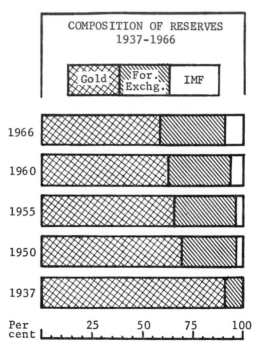

Such vast changes in the amount, the distribution, and the structure of reserves could not have occurred unless the United States was willing to accept an impairment of its reserve position and other countries were willing to accumulate reserves, particularly in dollars. Until 1958, the United States regarded its balance of payments as subordinate to other objectives of its international economic policy, such as the reconstruction of Europe and the reconstitution of the monetary reserves of these countries. Thus the United States continued Marshall Plan aid even while the recipients were adding substantial amounts of gold and dollars to their reserves. After 1958, the United States did regard the restoration of its balance of payments as of major importance. The U.S. surplus on goods and services was increased to $8.5 billion in 1964. But this improvement in the trade and service accounts was partly offset by an increase in U.S. private foreign investment. In the past two years, the investment boom and large military expenditures for Vietnam have prevented further progress in eliminating the U.S. payments deficit.

The U.S. balance of payments provided the surplus countries of continental Europe the opportunity of restoring their reserves. Until a few years ago, there could be no doubt of their need for a substantial increase in their reserves. More recently, they have been reluctant to see a continuation of the U.S. payments deficit. This is not because their reserves are excessive or because they are growing at a too rapid rate. It would be difficult to specify which European countries have more reserves than they need. Rather, their concern with domestic inflationary pressures has made them unwilling to see a continuation of their payments surpluses and of U.S. payments deficits.

The industrial countries of continental Europe have an inflation problem. It is an exaggeration, however, to attribute their rising prices and costs in any significant degree to the U.S. payments deficit. In the last twelve years, the Common Market countries, Switzerland, and Austria had net exports of goods and services averaging about 0.7 per cent of their gross national product. Such a modest diversion of resources for the acquisition of reserves cannot be regarded as a major factor in European inflation. In this same period, the United States has had a continuous surplus in net exports of goods and services and has provided the rest of the world with real resources out of its own production.

More emphasis appears to be placed on the inflationary effects of the U.S. payments deficits through the monetary expansion induced in the surplus countries. A balance-of-payments surplus, measured on a reserve transactions basis, automatically increases the money supply. The authorities may offset the influx of money by countermeasures, they may permit the influx to increase the money supply but prevent a further expansion of credit, or they may permit the influx to generate a multiple expansion of credit. If the monetary authorities are willing to permit an expansion of credit, and do not offset or minimize the effect of an influx of monetary reserves, the banking base that these reserves provide for credit expansion is only a substitute for the acquisition of other assets by the central bank. In quantitative terms, the acquisition of reserves accounted for only a small part of the increase in the monetary assets in most European countries during the past five years. In the seven countries below, the median proportion of the increase in monetary assets in the form of monetary reserves was 9.1 per cent of the total.

SOURCES OF INCREASE IN MONETARY ASSETS
IN EUROPEAN COUNTRIES, 1961–66
(Billions of domestic monetary units)

Country	Monetary assets June 30, 1961*	Monetary assets June 30, 1966*	Increase	Sources of increase Reserves	Credit
Austria	90.21	158.62	68.41	13.49	54.92
Belgium	285.60	438.60	153.00	25.10	127.90
France	108.21	201.41	93.20	21.03	72.17
Germany	183.50	323.30	139.80	6.70	133.10
Italy	14,582.00	28,027.00	13,445.00	1,222.00	12,223.00
Netherlands	19.20	29.47	10.27	0.22	10.04
Switzerland	51.73	79.98	28.25	2.55	25.71

* Currency, current deposits, time and savings deposits, and other banking items. Source: *International Financial Statistics*, Supplement to 1966/67 and January, 1967.

The present reserve system has reached a turning point. In the past two years, the amount of reserves held in the form of dollars has declined. In part, this has been due to the smaller U.S. payments deficit. In part, it has been due to the conversion of dollars into gold. It is evident that dollars cannot contribute to the growth of monetary reserves, at least for some time and certainly not again on the scale of the past. The accumulation of reserve liabilities at a rapid rate exposes the United States to the danger of massive conversions of dollars into gold at a time of political or economic crisis. In any event, the rest of the world cannot continue to depend on the U.S. balance of payments as a source of reserves. Once the U.S. payments deficit is eliminated, the world will have no other means of adding to its reserves except from the newly mined gold and the gold sales of the Soviet Union that are not absorbed by industrial production and private hoarding. This is much too small and far too uncertain for the world's monetary needs.

Professor Triffin has suggested that the present holdings of dollars and sterling by foreign governments and central banks be funded. His purpose is to avoid the danger of a flight from dollars and sterling into gold. The funding of dollars and sterling would impose deflationary forces on the world economy through the obligation to liquidate the debt. Moreover, it would cause a sharp and immediate reduction in total monetary reserves. The world needs reserves in the form of foreign exchange. They are a useful and necessary component of monetary reserves in a world in which central banks have replaced private gold and foreign exchange arbitrage in the regulation of the exchange market. Whatever arrangements are made for reforming the reserve system, a considerable part of reserves will continue to be in the form of dollars and sterling. Nevertheless, it is neither possible nor desirable to depend on foreign exchange for a major part of the future growth in monetary reserves.

CREATION OF A NEW RESERVE ASSET

Neither gold nor foreign exchange can provide an assured and adequate growth of monetary reserves. This is inherent in the conditions that determine the increment of such assets in monetary reserves. Furthermore, because these conditions change rapidly, there is enormous year to year variability in the growth of gold and foreign exchange reserves. As a consequence, monetary reserves may increase enormously in some years (1950, 1960, 1963), while they may increase very little or actually decline in other years (1957, 1959, 1966). This is shown in Chart VI-4.

The variability in the year-to-year growth in gold reserves is not due to rapid changes in output. Gold production in recent years has risen at a relatively steady rate. Similarly, the industrial consumption of gold has also risen steadily, but at a very rapid rate. On the other hand, the other factors that affect the flow of gold into monetary reserves are highly volatile. Gold sales of the Soviet Union depend on its balance of payments, and year-to-year

Chart VI-4

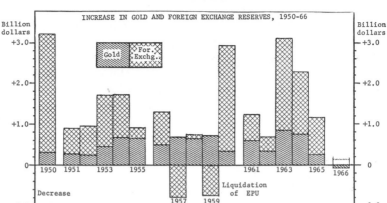

changes are due primarily to extraordinary import needs, such as grain imports when there is a crop failure. The greatest volatility, however, is in the absorption of gold in private hoards, in speculation, and in monetary reserves of Communist countries, such as China. As a consequence, the annual increment in the monetary gold stock in the past ten years has ranged from a high of about $840 million in 1963 to a low of about $240 million in 1965 and an actual decline in 1966. In the past six years, the average annual increase in the monetary gold stock outside the Communist bloc, but including holdings of the IMF and other international institutions, was less than $450 million.

The growth of monetary reserves in the form of foreign exchange is even more variable. The principal determinant of the growth of foreign exchange reserves since 1950 has been the U.S. balance of payments on a reserve transactions basis. From 1951 to 1957, the U.S. deficit averaged $600 million a year, and the balance of payments was in surplus in 1951 and 1957. From 1958 to 1966, the U.S. deficit averaged nearly $2 billion a year, but the average fell to about $1 billion a year from 1964 to 1966. Furthermore, the effect of a U.S. deficit on reserves depends on the preference of the surplus countries for accumulating gold or dollars. As a consequence, there may be no growth of reserves in the form of dollars in some years. This was true in 1951, 1957, 1965, and 1966. For all forms of foreign exchange, the annual change in reserves has ranged between an increase of $2.9 billion in 1950 and $2.3 billion in 1963, to a decrease of $800 million in 1956 and of $735 million in 1959 (incident to the liquidation of the EPU) and virtually no change in 1966.

For the future, there is no reason to expect a larger growth of gold reserves than in the past, and there may be no growth whatever in the next few years. On foreign exchange reserves, there is considerable reason for expecting a much smaller growth in the future, and little or no growth in dollar reserves in the next few years. The policy of the United States is to restore its balance of payments; and this will be accomplished. When U.S. payments are balanced, the increase in total reserves will be limited to newly mined gold and gold sales of the Soviet Union not absorbed in industrial uses and in private hoards. And when U.S. payments are in surplus, total monetary reserves, excluding gold-tranche claims on the IMF, may not grow at all, as the increase of gold reserves, if any, may be offset by a decrease in dollar reserves.

The world needs an adequate growth of monetary reserves at a relatively steady rate. As this cannot be supplied through gold or foreign exchange, it will have to be done through the creation of a new reserve asset. This new reserve asset will necessarily have a close resemblance to foreign exchange reserves; but it should also have some of the reserve characteristics of gold. That is to say, while the new reserve asset will inevitably be a credit instrument in the sense that it will be an obligation of the countries that create it, the new reserve asset should have a fixed and guaranteed gold value and it should be a final reserve asset.

The best way to provide for the orderly growth of reserves is through the creation of Reserve Units. The members of the IMF would establish a subsidiary, say the Reserve Unit Account, authorized to issue Reserve Units backed by the currencies of the participating countries, each member depositing an agreed amount of its own currency in the Reserve Unit Account in return for an equivalent amount of Reserve Units. Thus, if the United States should be allotted $300 million of Reserve Units, it would deposit the same amount of dollars, guaranteed against depreciation, with the Reserve Unit Account. The allotment of Re-

serve Units to participating countries could be in proportion
to their quotas in the IMF or on a similar basis. The participating countries would undertake to accept Reserve Units in
balance-of-payments settlements.

The Reserve Unit would be a composite foreign exchange
asset composed in determined proportions of all of the currencies of the participating countries. As by far the greater
part of the backing of the Reserve Unit would consist of
dollars, sterling, marks, francs, and the currencies of other
countries of the very highest credit standing, it would be
exceptionally well secured. Furthermore, the IMF could use
its accumulated surplus to underwrite any loss that might
be incurred when a participating country withdraws from
the Reserve Unit arrangements. It would also be possible
for the Group of Ten to guarantee its own members against
any loss from the holding of Reserve Units by sharing the
risk among themselves.

The amount of Reserve Units issued each year should be
sufficient, with the average increment of monetary gold, to
provide for an adequate but not excessive increase in total
monetary reserves. As the issue of Reserve Units would be
exclusively for the purpose of assuring the normal trend
growth of aggregate reserves, it would be possible to determine the amount of the annual issue for a period five years
ahead. If for some reason the agreed amount to be issued in
a given year should appear to be too large or too small, the
actual issue of that year could be increased or decreased by
a special vote of the participating countries.

The Reserve Unit proposal has been criticized as a dangerous innovation because it would provide countries with
reserves that they do not earn. This seems to be based on a
misapprehension of how countries acquire reserves under
the present system. In fact, countries add to their reserves
through a balance-of-payments surplus. That surplus may
be earned, in the sense that a country has an excess of
receipts over payments for goods and services. But a surplus may also arise from borrowing or some other capital
inflow. That is not earned in the usual sense, although a
country does transfer valuable assets (securities, claims,
etc.) in return for the capital it receives. The Reserve Unit
is simply a multilateral credit in the form of reserve assets
provided by all the participating countries to each other. In

return for the Reserve Units they receive, the participating countries must give an equivalent value in their own currencies.

I do not see how the Reserve Unit proposal differs in this respect from the reserves that would be created by a world central bank of the kind that Triffin has in mind. If such a central bank were to extend reserve credit to a country with a balance-of-payments deficit, it would be giving the borrowing country reserve assets that it did not earn, but it would be in return for a valuable claim. Similarly, if a world central bank were to provide countries with reserves through open-market operations, it would be giving these countries reserve assets that they did not earn, but it would be in return for a valuable claim.

The essential difference between reserves created under the Triffin Plan and under the Reserve Unit proposal is that the amount created by a world central bank would be indeterminate, depending on the credit operations that the world central bank decided to undertake. Insofar as the reserves are created in response to requests from credits by countries, the actual growth of reserves would depend on the balance-of-payments deficits to be financed. In a period when the world pattern of payments is well balanced, no reserves would be created through the extension of credits to deficit countries. And if a country that previously borrowed from the world central bank were to repay its credits, aggregate reserves would be reduced. On the other hand, if the world central bank were to undertake open-market operations in order to create reserve assets, it would be the same as an issue of Reserve Units except for the fact that there would be an *ad hoc* determination of the amount of open-market operations and no assurance of how they would be distributed country by country. The philosophy of the Triffin Plan would indicate that the amount to be created would be related to the immediate need for reserves to meet balance-of-payments deficits.

The philosophy of the Reserve Unit proposal is quite different. The issue of such reserves is not intended to enable a country to raise the average level of its imports and other payments relative to its exports and other receipts— that is, to have a more adverse balance of payments over a period of years than it would otherwise have. The purpose of the Reserve Unit proposal is to enable countries to have a normal growth of both exports (receipts) and imports (payments), but not to change the relationship between them. This does not mean that Reserve Units are not to be used to finance a balance-of-payments deficit. That is, in fact, their function in the short run. But Reserve Units are reserves and not capital inflow; and as reserves, it is expected that each country that has drawn down its Reserve Units will in proper time restore its holdings in the same way as it would restore its reserves.

Despite this, it may be asked whether countries will treat Reserve Units as an increment of reserves or as a windfall inflow of foreign capital. No doubt, some countries hardpressed for capital to finance development will use their allocation of Reserve Units in this way. To the extent that this occurs, the Reserve Units would be concentrated in larger part in the reserves of other countries. If this should happen, it would be a justification for reducing the annual increment to total reserves in the form of Reserve Units, as the amount necessary for the normal growth of the reserves of all other countries could then be supplied with a smaller annual issue. As the few countries that might follow such a policy are likely to have relatively small allocations of Reserve Units, their attitude toward reserves cannot have significant consequences for the world economy.

The more important question is whether the great industrial countries will regard the Reserve Units allocated to them as a normal part of their reserves—to be used when necessary to meet a payments deficit, but to be restored to their reserves in due time. The fear that countries like the United States or the United Kingdom would use the Reserve Units allocated to them to perpetuate a balance-of-payments deficit is groundless. For the United States, the allocation of Reserve Units might be on the order of $300 million a year. Such an annual allocation of Reserve Units would be of marginal significance in financing a U.S. payments deficit if it should persist for some time. The fact is that the United States and the United Kingdom have a deficiency of reserves; and their policy will have to be to accumulate Reserve Units in order to restore their reserves. Nevertheless, it is worth stressing that the the Reserve Unit system will not achieve its objectives unless the great industrial countries maintain a well-balanced pattern of international payments. Obviously, this does not preclude occasional deficits and surpluses, particularly in response to cyclical fluctuations, but it does require that there should not be large and persistent deficits or surpluses.

ROLE OF GOLD IN THE FUTURE

Even if the Reserve Unit proposal is adopted, gold will continue to have a central role in the international monetary system. There are two reasons for this. First, the historical role of gold as the basis for money is so well established that confidence in Reserve Units will for a long time depend on assurance of its full equivalence to gold. Second, because gold constitutes the greater part of total monetary reserves, there is no way of meeting the reserve needs of the world except by continuing to hold gold in reserves and by continuing to use gold in international settlements. In fact, the same argument can be applied to dollars and sterling. The termination of the holding and use of these currencies as reserves would create a critical shortage of monetary reserves.

In a reserve system using gold, foreign exchange, and Reserve Units, it is necessary to maintain the equivalent attractiveness of these assets—in holding them as reserves and in using them for balance-of-payments settlements. The analogy with dollars as monetary reserves may help to clarify the problem of establishing Reserve Units as an acceptable reserve asset capable of performing the function of reserves. The equivalence of dollars with gold is assured in the first instance by maintaining convertibility of dollars into gold at 35 an ounce. In addition, countries find it attractive to hold dollars because such reserves can be invested in the U.S. money market and thus earn a considerable return. Ultimately, however, the equivalence of dollars and gold depends on the maintenance of a strong payments position by the United States, so that the growth of dollar reserves is limited to the amount that countries wish to hold without large net conversions into gold.

Some of these principles can be applied to Reserve Units. The first, to limit the amount of Reserve Units issued, is indispensable and presents no difficulty. If the growth of total reserves in the form of gold, dollars, and Reserve Units is moderate, the willingness to hold all forms of reserves will be greater. The payment of interest on Reserve Units, to make them a more attractive form of reserves, presents greater difficulty. As Reserve Units would be a credit instrument, involving the transfer of real resources or capital assets from a surplus country to a deficit country, a case can be made for the payment of a moderate rate of interest on net holdings of Reserve Units. The rate would have to be low, so that while the Reserve Unit would be more attractive relative to gold, it would not be too attractive relative to foreign exchange. Furthermore, it would be desirable to keep the interest rate on Reserve Units fixed for long periods, instead of varying with money market rates, in order to give the reserve centers greater freedom in using monetary policy to maintain the attractiveness of the reserve currencies.

The objective should be to give maximum freedom in the use of Reserve Units in balance-of-payments settlements without letting them degenerate into an inferior reserve asset. Obviously, it is not possible to make Reserve Units convertible into gold. If Reserve Units were subject to this obligation they would lose the characteristic of being a final reserve asset. The first rule must be that countries should not use Reserve Units merely to change the composition of their reserves—that is, to secure indirect conversion of Reserve Units into gold. Beyond this, it would be necessary to give unlimited acceptability to Reserve Units in settlement by deficit countries without relegating gold to a sacred but inactive role. If gold were seldom, or never, used it would create the impression that gold is too valuable to be used in balance-of-payments settlements except in time of crisis.

One way in which the unlimited acceptability of Reserve Units could be established would be by linking the use of Reserve Units with gold (or gold and foreign exchange reserves). A surplus country would have no fear of acquiring an excessive amount of Reserve Units if deficit countries at the same time had to use their other reserves in balance of payments settlements. There is implicit in this the view that deficit countries would regard a decline in their Reserve Unit holdings as more tolerable than a decline in their gold and dollar reserves, and that surplus countries would regard a rise in their Reserve Unit holdings as less acceptable than a rise in their gold and dollar reserves. This may not prove to be so, particularly if the growth of aggregate reserves is moderate. Nevertheless, it is understandable that until confidence in Reserve Units is firmly established, a *de facto* equivalence of Reserve Units with gold and dollars could be secured by linking their use in international settlements. Among a small group of participating countries, the link with gold (or gold and foreign exchange) could be a helpful safeguard against the risk of excessive acquisition of Reserve Units by one or a few surplus countries. With more than 100 participating countries, the linking of Reserve Units with gold (or gold and foreign exchange) in settlements would create almost insuperable administrative difficulties.

An alternative safeguard would be to limit the obligation of countries to hold Reserve Units without limiting their acceptability in international settlements. This would require countries to accept all of the Reserve Units that come to them in balance of payments settlements, but would permit them to convert the excess above a holding limit into gold. Thus, a deficit country would be assured that it could always use the Reserve Units it has in settlements with any country, even if that country already holds the prescribed limit. At the same time, a surplus country would be assured that it could not be compelled to hold more Reserve Units than the agreed maximum, unless it chooses to do so.

There are two types of holding limit that could be established. For example, the holding limit on Reserve Units could be made a multiple (say, three times) of a country's cumulative allocation of Reserve Units. That is to say, the maximum net acquisition of Reserve Units by a surplus country would be twice the amount of its allocations. An alternative would be to relate the holding limit on Reserve Units to the amount of other reserves (gold and foreign exchange) that a country holds. Thus, the holding limit could be one-half as much as a country's other reserve assets. Such a holding limit would not be absolute, as it would rise whenever a surplus country acquires gold and foreign exchange reserves.

If a holding limit is established on Reserve Units, some means must be provided for converting the excess which a surplus country accepts in balance-of-payments settlements. The conversion could not be in other national currencies (not even those of the Group of Ten), for unless these currencies could be converted into gold, there would be no effective limit on the Reserve Units plus currencies that a surplus country would be obligated to acquire and hold. The conversion, if it is to serve as a limitation, would have to be in gold. The obligation to provide gold for such conversion could be shared by all participating countries or by the deficit countries—that is, those that have drawn down their allocations of Reserve Units. To determine the liability of each of more than 100 countries in providing gold for conversion of excessive holding of Reserve Units would present great administrative difficulties. Alternatively, the Group of Ten could agree to provide on an equitable basis whatever gold is necessary for the conversion of excessive holding of Reserve Units. A country providing gold for this purpose would, of course, receive Reserve Units in return.

There are some people that believe that such safeguards are unnecessary and that they will ultimately be abandoned. In my opinion, the Reserve Unit will in time come to be recognized as a reserve asset fully equivalent to gold and dollars. At the same time, such limitations have a practical use. There is widespread faith in the power of gold to impose balance-of-payments discipline on deficit countries. Even with the use of Reserve Units in international payments, gold will continue to perform that function, although in a much less restrictive manner. In a very real sense, gold will remain the principal determinant of the behavior of the world payments system, whether this is done through linking the use of Reserve Units with gold (or gold and foreign exchange) or through holding limits in which excess Reserve Units are converted into gold. That is why such a payments system of gold, foreign exchange, and Reserve Units can properly be regarded as a form of the gold standard.

There will be those who will argue that this is not the gold standard. In fact, the development of the Reserve Unit as a new reserve asset is no different from the development of bank notes or bank deposits as new forms of money under the classical gold standard. The gold standard has shown great adaptability, and that is why it has remained the basis for the international payments system. The only way we can keep the gold standard is by enabling it to evolve to meet the needs of the time. That is how the gold standard survived up to now; that is how it can survive from now on.

The new gold standard, as I conceive it, would have three basic features: First, the parities of all currencies would be fixed in terms of gold and these parities would not be changed, except after consultation with the IMF. Second, the role of gold in international settlements would be continued, but the excessive reliance on gold as the only final reserve asset would be moderated. Third, while retaining gold and foreign exchange as reserves, a new reserve asset, the Reserve Unit, with a guaranteed gold value, would be created and issued gradually and in moderate amounts, to be used with gold and foreign exchange in international settlements. Such a reserve system would assure the capacity of the gold standard to function effectively, without the restrictive effects of an inadequate growth of reserves and without the disruptive effects of reducing the gold value of currencies.

CHAPTER VII

EXCHANGE OF VIEWS

A most rewarding feature of the Bologna Center conference was a session entirely devoted to an exchange of views by the authors of the three most influential approaches to international monetary reform. It was the aim of the chairman, Willard L. Thorp, to reveal specific points of difference as well as broad areas of agreement and, in particular, to avoid a sterile *dialogue de sourds.* In this objective he succeeded to a remarkable degree and achieved, not a consensus—certainly not a consensus on policy—but a genuine meeting of minds. The dialogue below is taken directly from the tape recording.

R. H.

Chairman THORP:* This morning, we are about to have what we call in the OECD a "confrontation." We shall begin by asking the individuals who are associated with the different approaches to discuss together what they feel are the main points on which they disagree. I would like to start the dialogue by pointing out what seems to be a difference in emphasis between Mr. Rueff, on the one hand, and Messrs. Triffin and Bernstein, on the other. It appears to me that Mr. Rueff has addressed himself primarily to what he feels is an excessive accumulation of non-gold reserves; and he has proposed a way in which gold could be substituted for the existing paper reserves. Presumably, if his proposal

---

* Achieving early fame as an economist, Willard L. Thorp has been equally prominent in a variety of official positions. At Amherst College he has served as professor of economics, as a trustee, for a time as acting president, and as director of the Merrill Center for Economics, where his skill in organizing and chairing conferences of world experts on various subjects earned wide praise. He played a prominent role in the Marshall Plan as Assistant Secretary of State for Economic Affairs, and is currently chairman of the OECD Development Assistance Committee in Paris. Among his books are *Business Annals, Trade, Aid, or What?,* and *The New Inflation,* of which he is coauthor.

were adopted, the system would operate as the old gold standard operated and, according to his exposition yesterday, his reform appears to be a one-time operation, with certain commitments concerning how governments would behave thereafter. On the other hand, both Mr. Bernstein and Mr. Triffin seem to be concerned primarily with the problem of how to achieve a gradual increase in reserves, and have proposed two different ways in which this gradual increase could take place. Neither of them appears to be much concerned with the present character of the reserves, nor to feel that something has to be done in the way of shifting the composition. I am not sure whether I am correctly stating a disagreement, but this seems to me an interesting point to pursue. I would therefore like to ask the participants if they would be willing to begin by clarifying what seems to me a difference in yesterday's presentations.

EDWARD M. BERNSTEIN: Only one of your remarks needs a minor qualification. First, Bob [Triffin] is very much worried about the composition of reserves, and would do something about it. I am not worried about the composition of reserves, but I recognize that there is a problem in having so little gold, which is a final reserve asset, and having so much foreign exchange, which is by its terms convertible into gold. As I said, Bob would change the composition of reserves by taking out some of this foreign exchange. I would try to establish something like a fixed fiduciary issue with the existing foreign exchange. I have no desire—and I have some fear—about increasing it. But I would make the new Reserve Unit equivalent to gold in the sense of being a final reserve asset. This is the only qualification of your summary that I would suggest.

Chairman THORP: Have I correctly represented you, Mr. Rueff?

JACQUES RUEFF: Yes, you are perfectly right in stating that I am afraid of the accumulation of non-gold reserves, and I do want to replace them—as reserves. Let me say a word about the essential difference between what Triffin would like to do and what I would like to do. Triffin is chiefly interested, if I am right, in a 3 to 4 per cent increase in reserves to accommodate the growth of international trade. The essence of my proposal, on the other hand, is to replace the non-gold reserves, as you say, by gold. You are quite right in saying that this is a one-time operation. The problem, as I see it, is to liquidate the effect of World War II. The effect of World War I in the monetary field was liquidated in the Great Depression. What I would like to do is to make sure that World War II—and fifteen years of the gold-exchange standard—will not be liquidated by another great depression. That is why I am looking for a special procedure, after which the system should work without further new operations of this kind unless there is another world war, or the re-establishment of the gold-exchange standard, or the discovery of new techniques or new gold mines that would greatly reduce the cost of producing gold.

The last point you mentioned, Mr. Chairman, was that I do not appear to be concerned with the need for a gradual increase in reserves. I would state the matter differently. I consider that there is a great deal of flexibility in the working of the gold standard. In the last century, for example, there was an enormous increase in trade, and it was met by the gold standard.

Chairman THORP: I think we should now ask our panel to start asking questions. Mr. Bernstein, would you like to begin?

BERNSTEIN: I want to ask Professor Rueff whether he is disturbed in any way at an increase in the recorded value of the gold reserves of the Western countries by $41 billion all at once. Are you disturbed by the enormous and sudden increase in the total amount of reserves, even after you pay off the official dollars owed by the United States?

RUEFF: I am not afraid of such an increase. In my statement I recommended various uses of the increase in the nominal value of gold reserves—the repayment of dollar balances and sterling balances, a loan to Great Britain, loans to developing countries, the repayment of debt—and if these things were done, there should be no danger of surplus reserves. Again I must say that the essential feature of my proposal is that it would remove a dangerous situation inherited from the past. It is not intended to meet the need for a regular increase in reserves corresponding to the increase in trade, because I consider that money is a result, not a cause. It is created according to need by the various mechanisms of flexibility which are built into the monetary system. The basic flexibility is the flexibility of credit creation, which has immense potentiality. But beyond that is the flexibility of gold production, as influenced by the general movement of prices.

BERNSTEIN: You are not afraid of the credit creation potentiality on top of the $19 billion increase in the dollar value of its gold that Continental Europe will get?

RUEFF: You mean the reserves?

BERNSTEIN: I am worried about several things, but not basically about the question of how flexible the credit creation system is. What I want to know is this: We have $41 billion in gold, $19 billion of it in Continental Europe. Double the price and you have $82 billion, of which Continental Europe has $38 billion. There is then a flow of gold from the United States to the countries that have official dollar reserves, so that the United States has about what it started with, and the other countries, including Europe, have much more. I wonder whether you are not disturbed about suddenly taking the quantity of reserves in the world in the form of gold and saying, "Once we put it on the books at $41 billion, and we behaved as if it were $41 billion—but now it is $82 billion." What if people behave as if it were $82 billion? That does not disturb you?

RUEFF: Not if the increase in reserves is properly handled. Again, I say, the principal use ought to be the repayment of the official dollar balances and of such sterling balances as the British government deems fit to repay. As for the rest, it is easy to find, I think, many uses, such as I have proposed; and if after that there were signs of inflation, I would point out that inflation is much easier to cure than deflation. There is no direct connection between the stock of gold and the amount of credit; we have all seen that gold reserves have varied quite a lot in various countries without disturbances of the same magnitude in the money supply. I am sure you would agree that it is very easy for a central bank to cancel the internal effect of an inflow of gold. Nothing is easier than to sterilize gold. For instance, when you have an influx of gold, you can cancel the effect on the money supply through open-market operations. I don't think there is an important danger there.

ROBERT TRIFFIN: May I put the same question somewhat differently, Mr. Rueff? I would like to hear the evidence for your conclusion that gold production rises much more in a period of declining prices. Looking at the historical record, the period of enormous increase in gold production was, of course, from 1849 to 1872—that is, a period of *rising* prices. For the major countries on the gold standard during that period, gold production increased at an average annual rate of 6.2 per cent. In the period that followed, 1873 to 1892, which was a period of *declining* prices, gold production increased at an average rate of 1.4 per cent a year instead of 6.2 per cent. I fail to discern in those figures the impact of the incentive that lower prices gave to an increase in gold production. It may have come later, but only after twenty years, which is a long time. During that period, whatever stability was exhibited by the system was really due to changes in credit creation. The total money supply for those countries increased at an average rate of about 4 per cent a year in the first period and at an average rate of about 3 per cent a year in the second. There was a fluctuation, but a much smaller fluctuation than would have come from gold alone.

This in a sense confirms what you said—that there are *other* factors which can offset the undesirable fluctuations which gold alone would impart to the system. But it seems to me that the major argument in favor of your system—which I fully appreciate—is its automaticity. As soon as one recognizes that the automaticity has to be corrected by various forms of monetary management, however, the main merit of the system disappears.

Concerning the present situation, I agree with Mr. Bernstein. I have always been very much surprised that a man as concerned with inflation as you are could view with equanimity the flood of inflation that might result if the doubling of the price of gold really were to have automatic consequences. Your remedy is to suggest a number of agreements which would be far more difficult to negotiate than the initial doubling of the price of gold! You want an agreement simultaneous with the revaluation of gold that, from then on, national currencies will no longer be used as reserves. You also want an agreement that we in the United States will use our revaluation profits to repay our debts to central banks, and an agreement that other countries will use their revaluation profits to repay the debts of Britain. All this involves quite a few agreements, and, if these agreements do not accompany the doubling of the price of gold, the situation will be extremely dangerous indeed.

Even if we suppose that all this is accomplished—which I think takes a great deal of optimism—it is quite possible that, as a consequence, there would be an enormous disgorging of the gold hoards which have accumulated over the past few years. As you know, in the early 1930s there was a disgorging of $2 billion. I think that if the price of gold were doubled today, the disgorging by private individuals would amount to much more than $2 billion, because the amount of gold is much larger than it was then. How will you take care of that?

But let us come back to the main point. Let us assume that the price of gold is doubled—that is to say, that the dollar has been devalued by 50 per cent in terms of gold. I think that in this case many central banks would feel that, at the new price, the dollar would be safe at least for a while, that there would not be a new devaluation within the next few years—and, indeed, that is the way you would want them to feel. In these circumstances the central banks, which in recent months have begun to liquidate their foreign exchange at an alarming rate, would again begin to accumulate dollar reserves. I think that your proposal, if not accompanied by a definite and general renunciation of the use of national currencies as reserves, would give a new lease on life to the gold-exchange standard. An essential part of your plan—and the part with which I agree—is that the use of national currencies as international reserves should be limited to working balances. But I think the impact of your plan would be exactly the opposite; it would give a new attractiveness to dollar balances or to sterling balances after devaluation.

RUEFF: If I am right, I see three questions: first, the need for an agreement and the chance of it being negotiated; second, the need for flexibility; and third, the question of automaticity.

TRIFFIN: Also the question of the impact of changes in the price level on the production of gold. May I add one point on that, by the way? The reason why the money supply grew so smoothly over the periods of gold avalanche and of gold shortage is that during the period in which gold was produced in great abundance, 80 per cent of it went directly into public circulation and only 20 per cent into reserves, whereas during the following period of gold shortage, the situation was exactly the reverse: 20 per cent went into circulation and 80 per cent went into central banks. It was mainly this development that smoothed out the general monetary impact.

RUEFF: Let me return to your point about the need for an agreement. You consider that this is very difficult and unlikely. Let me say that the main thing which has to be agreed is that no new dollar or sterling balances will be used to create money. This is only a return to a situation which existed for a century. Until 1914 it was quite inconceivable for central banks to use foreign assets to create money. In those days the gold-exchange standard had been applied only to a few colonial countries for which the mother country was responsible and whose behavior could, if I may say so, be controlled by the mother country. But a system like the modern gold-exchange standard, which involves as a consequence that a debtor country immediately recovers what the creditor country has received, is not only childish; it is absurd.

TRIFFIN: But that is what happened when Roosevelt raised the price of gold; after two or three years, the central banks began to accumulate dollars and sterling all over again.

RUEFF: Well, to a small degree.

TRIFFIN: No, not to a small degree—I can give you the figures.

BERNSTEIN: Yes, in sterling; the accumulation was not overwhelming in dollars. The total was around $5 billion for both dollars and sterling—$6 billion according to your figures, Bob. But anyway, I do not think we ought to doubt the capacity of a group of countries which can make such a change in the price of gold, also to make a binding agreement on further holdings of dollars and sterling as reserves. I would not put this down as an impossible obstacle. I know of many greater ones, and I would put this rather low on the list. But I am disturbed by the notion that if you have a monetary system in which increments of reserves have to depend on so many uncertain factors—(a) gold production, (b) gold sales into the system from outside countries like the Soviet Union, (c) industrial consumption, (d) private hoards which can be positive or negative—you can nevertheless expect to have a smooth growth of reserves: one which will not give us the kind of price fluctuations we had when there was no gold-exchange standard except in Java and in the Philippines and in India. What would be your comment on that?

RUEFF: I am glad you asked that question, because it raises the whole subject of automaticity. Contrary to Mr. Triffin, who says that the system I propose has the great merit of automaticity, I really never have believed that a monetary system is automatic. Just the reverse. I consider, for instance, that the composition of the assets of a central bank depends entirely on its own policy—which means the level at which it sets the discount rate in relation to the rates in the market. You may immediately say that this or that country uses open-market operations instead of the discount rate, but the theory is just the same: in open-market operations the central bank goes into the market at a certain rate instead of the market going to the central bank. Now you have in the assets of the central bank— against credits and money—gold and bills. It depends only on the will of the central bank, by setting its discount rate at a proper level, to replace all the bills with gold. This gives an enormous margin of flexibility.

I have never thought, and I have never observed, that the administration of a central bank is automatic; and I do not consider the gold standard automatic. It is a device, something like a motor car: you give the driver a brake and an accelerator; he must use the brake and he must use the accelerator, and it is a conscious management. That is why I am not afraid of dishoarding. If the brake and the accelerator are used in a wise manner, nothing is easier for the central bank, provided it wants to do so, than to cancel an excess of availability. Of course, it is much more difficult to deal with recession, because, as Keynes said, it is easy to lead a horse to water, but you can't make him drink. It is much easier to prevent him from drinking, and that sort of operation can be done by the central bank.

TRIFFIN: May I comment? I am very grateful for this precision, which helps me to correct what I had misunderstood in your proposal. I would certainly agree that central banks *can* offset the disturbances which your plan would introduce. But it is not quite as easy as it sounds, as there are certain types of credit flows which are rather essential for a smooth functioning of the economy, and if, suddenly, because of large-scale dishoarding, the banking system has to contract its normal rate of lending in order to offset that impact, the result may be very disturbing. I do agree that it can be done, but I do not see much point in introducing these $41 billion in new reserves in order then to sterilize them.

RUEFF: If I were in favor of the Triffin Plan, I would see no point whatever, but it is because I am afraid of certain consequences of that plan that I think it is necessary to try to find something else. I think the so-called rigidity of habits in the monetary field is immensely exaggerated. I have had some practice in central banking. There are quite a few traditions which have been changed overnight, and the policies called for by my proposals would not need to be introduced overnight; they could be introduced gradually.

BERNSTEIN: One more question and I will be through. What is so much better about taking a bar of gold weighing 400 ounces and now valued at $14,000, crossing out the $14,000 and making it $28,000; instead of keeping this $14,000 bar of gold as it is and creating along with it a packet of currency (dollars, sterling, marks, francs, and so on) which are now also worth $14,000, and saying, "Here are $28,000 of reserves"? Why is it better to take the bar of gold and say, "Once $14,000 but now $28,000," instead of keeping the gold bar at $14,000 and adding a Reserve Unit which is gold-guaranteed, which is a final reserve asset—you cannot run away from it—and which has an equivalent amount in currencies behind it? Why is your scheme better?

RUEFF: I am delighted with your question and very grateful, because it shows the extraordinary similarity between your plan and the plan to increase the price of gold. Creating more reserves against gold and in proportion to gold is—you are quite right—exactly . . .

BERNSTEIN: No, reserves under my plan are not created in proportion to gold; sorry.

RUEFF: Well, then, let us speak of the CRU [the French proposal for a "Composite Reserve Unit"], which was an illegitimate child of your plan. The CRU involved a creation of reserves in proportion to the amount of gold. May I say, with all due politeness, that this is a hypocritical way of changing the price of gold.

BERNSTEIN: I think you ought to talk, not about the CRU, which even the Group of Ten is no longer considering, but about my proposal for a Reserve Unit.

RUEFF: Of course the CRU is not the question. But your plan is not quite clear. Your speech of yesterday was so wonderfully subtle and full of nuances that, if I may say so, I was unable to see clearly on what basis you would create these supplementary reserves.

BERNSTEIN: I am very eager to answer your question, but I want to give you a chance to answer mine—not on the basis of the CRU, as proposed by the French, but on the basis of the Reserve Unit I have suggested. That is to say, a Reserve Unit where, say, the amount created each year is $1 billion, and where gold either may be used by itself or may be used along with Reserve Units. The Reserve Units created would not depend on the amount of gold that exists; their distribution would not depend on how much gold a country owns; and their use would not depend on the ratio of the total amount of gold to the total amount of Reserve Units. And if France, for example, having joined such a system, were to change its mind and decide that, after all, it did not like to see dollars or sterling used internationally, did not like to see even a collection of many currencies so used, and were to say, "We will step out"—in that case, the French would get back all the francs they had contributed to the Reserve Units, and, as for the rest, if they were creditors, they would get either gold or francs. So it isn't simply flimflam, as you are implying.

Now, to repeat, what I want to know is, why is it better to take a bar of gold and say that it is now $28,000, not $14,000, instead of simultaneously continuing to use gold but also using a new reserve asset, which is a final asset which cannot be converted into gold, so that you cannot escape from it?

TRIFFIN: Except if you withdraw.

BERNSTEIN: Except if you withdraw, and then of course the terms of liquidation are set out.

RUEFF: May I begin my answer with a question? The

asset will be used by debtor countries; what about creditor countries?

BERNSTEIN: Deficit countries and surplus countries. The deficit country presumably will be able, if it needs a particular currency to intervene in the foreign exchange market, to sell Reserve Units to, say, the Bank of France or the Federal Reserve Bank of New York in exchange for the currency which it then feeds into the market.

RUEFF: They would sell them to the central bank?

BERNSTEIN: Yes, just the way they sell a bar of gold. Or if you wish, I can put it another way: Countries could go on doing business just as they do now, but when they accumulate dollars, and a central bank has more than it wants, it presents them to the Federal Reserve Bank of New York, which says, "Yes, you are entitled to have the dollars converted into gold and Reserve Units. Here are your bars of gold and here is your claim on the Reserve Unit Account." And that is the settlement.

RUEFF: The Reserve Unit will be inconvertible unless a country leaves the system?

BERNSTEIN: That is right. I think it is fair to say that the Reserve Unit must be regarded as a final reserve asset. There may be provisions for protecting a country from being swamped with Reserve Units, but I think it is easier to start with the assumption that it is inconvertible. The mere holding of it does not give you a claim on gold.

RUEFF: That is the main point to which I object. I would like to explore this matter with both you and Triffin. I consider that issuing an inconvertible currency really destroys the mechanism through which we can hope for equilibrium in the balance of payments. My intention is to make that the central point of my question. I can ask it now, but maybe it is better to leave it.

BERNSTEIN: I think that if we are on this hot question now, we ought to continue with it.

Chairman THORP: Go ahead, ask your question.

RUEFF: I must say that it is a long question that I want to address to both my friends. I assume that the Triffin Plan, in its latest version which I have here, implies that the Triffin unit will be inconvertible. In his pamphlet—which I read with great interest—on the balance-of-payments and foreign investment position of the United States, Mr. Triffin writes that the proper long-term functioning of the international payments mechanism will necessarily entail some voluntary or agreed restraints on excessive hoarding of scarce gold metal as monetary reserves by individual countries and should, at the same time, provide countries with equally safe and more attractive media for liquid reserve holdings. That reminds me of a French minister of finance who wanted to issue a big loan, not to get money for his treasury, but to provide his friends with a good investment! Mr. Triffin writes later on that the agreements to be reached should encompass decisions among at least the major reserve holders regarding the use of national currencies, gold, and a new type of reserve asset in the future structure and creation of international reserves. So I think that both Mr. Bernstein's plan and Mr. Triffin's plan have in common some degree of inconvertibility. A country receiving payment from another country will not be free to request gold if it sees fit, but may have to keep some of its reserves in inconvertible form. This means that both Triffin and Bernstein would return to the situation in which the debtor country does not lose what the creditor country gains.

BERNSTEIN: No, I disagree with that.

RUEFF: Then will you explain? It seems to me that this new asset you are creating is a gift to the debtor country, which does not have to pay anything for it and therefore does not lose anything. Thus the incentive for balance disappears. I am probably wrong, but if you can explain I will appreciate it.

BERNSTEIN: I will try to explain. Suppose that the Reserve Units are created at a rate of $1 billion a year and allocated among all countries . . .

RUEFF: Allocated how?

BERNSTEIN: According to any formula you wish, but let's say according to the quotas in the International Monetary Fund. Suppose that out of the $1 billion, the United States gets $250 million in Reserve Units. For the $250 million the United States gets in Reserve Units, it gives in return an asset—a claim on the United States—which would be entirely liquidated if the United States were to leave the system and would be partially liquidated if a creditor country were to withdraw, as part of the creditor's reimbursement.

This $250 million therefore is, in a sense, a reserve acquired by the United States in exchange for a capital instrument—a credit instrument, if you wish—turned over by the United States to the Reserve Unit Account. The United States has in its reserves what it had before, as of the base date, and in the course of the year it gets this $250 million. If it now has a balance-of-payments deficit, its reserves go down and the reserves, say, of France, the creditor country, go up. For individual countries, the decline in one is the increase in the other; for the system as a whole, it is an annual investment of $1 billion a year.

Now may be a good time to answer the moral argument that is sometimes used as a criticism of the Reserve Unit proposal. Think of countries getting a reserve asset without first spending real resources to dig it out of the ground, refine it, ship it, and call it gold. Do you want the answer to this moral argument?

The argument doesn't disturb me at all. The notion that countries get reserves only by working is simply not true. Countries get reserves through a balance-of-payments surplus. That surplus is the end result of a collection of transactions involving goods, services, and capital. Canada is an excellent illustration for this purpose. Suppose Canada has an increase in reserves. If you want to say the Canadians "earned" it, I have no objection to your putting a label on a bit of their exports saying "This is how they got it"; but, if you go deeper, they acquired reserves because the capital inflow from the United States, including sale of Canadian bonds on the New York market, simply exceeded the current-account deficit they had. Now did they *earn* those reserves? Well, I do not like to use the word "earn" at all, but they did give something valuable for them. They either gave exports of goods or services, or instruments which yielded the purchasers abroad an income.

I can't see any difference between that and the Reserve Unit proposal. I certainly do not believe that it is good for the moral character of man to get something for nothing, without an equivalent obligation in return. If you want me to make that profession of faith, I'm prepared to make it, but I don't think it has much to do with economics.

Chairman THORP: Bob, do you want to answer Rueff's question?

TRIFFIN : Yes. Let me postpone my answer to what Mr. Bernstein has just said, because my argument is not simply a moral one in this case; it goes much further than that.

As far as Mr. Rueff's question is concerned, my answer is very different from that of Mr. Bernstein. In my own proposal, it is true that a country which is in balance-of-payments surplus agrees to accumulate this surplus partly in the form of a claim on, let us say, the International Monetary Fund, but this does not mean that the country which is in deficit receives any automatic loans from the International Monetary Fund—leaving aside the question of the outstanding dollar and sterling balances, which I deal with separately as a transitional problem. Under my plan, the country which is in deficit would have to pay for its deficit; there would be no automatic extension of credit to that country.

Suppose, for example, that the Bank of France has accumulated dollars because France has a surplus with the United States. The Bank of France would turn its dollars over to the IMF, and would receive in exchange a gold value deposit with the Fund. It would no longer hold the dollars, except for the working balances which it wished to hold and which were necessary for day-to-day intervention in the foreign exchange market. The U.S. deposit with the Fund would be reduced by the amount of dollars which France had turned over to the Fund, since the dollars are a debt of the United States. If the U.S. deposit were to fall below the minimum reserve requirement of the Triffin Plan, the United States, if it did not have other currencies to turn over to the Fund, would have to pay gold—except, of course, if the Fund, in its wisdom, were to decide by a collective decision of its membership that it wished to make an investment in the United States. But there would be no automatic credit to any debtor. There could be discretionary credits, as there are now in the Fund, but there would be no automatic credit.

BERNSTEIN : But there is no automatic credit to a debtor in my plan; there is an automatic allocation to everybody of a minor sum relative to total reserves and to balance-of-payments fluctuations. Any country which wants to get more than that has to have a balance-of-payments surplus.

Those which have a deficit are going to have less than that—and may have less of all their reserves.

TRIFFIN: May I mention one implication here, which is this: Each time you create $1 billion of new reserves, you are automatically committed to give $360 million of it to the United States and the United Kingdom. You are commited also to extend, probably, $250 million to $350 million to the less-developed countries. You have a very arbitrary allocation, based on an arbitrary system of quotas which would mean that you extend credits to these countries without taking into account the wisdom or the folly of the policies they are currently pursuing. I doubt very much whether such a system would survive for more than a few years.

BERNSTEIN: May I answer that, or is this something that Dr. Rueff should answer?

Chairman THORP: We have another voice that wants to come in; let us hear Mr. Gilbert.

MILTON GILBERT: Mr. Rueff has not yet answered one of Ed Bernstein's questions; may I answer it? I think it is quite an important question. The question was: Why do you want to raise the value of a bar of gold now worth $14,000 to $28,000, instead of keeping the gold at $14,000 and adding $14,000 of (say) Reserve Units? I do not want to say which is better; I only want to say why the two are different. This is important, because it is so often said that creating Reserve Units is a disguised way of raising the price of gold. But there is a fundamental difference, and that is in the effect on the gold market—that is to say, on the private demand for, and supply of, gold. In deciding on one approach or the other, the main point to be taken into account is just the difference in the effect on the gold market.

Chairman THORP: Let us set aside for the time being the whole question of gold supply and demand, because I am sure a number of people here can speak helpfully on that subject. This is certainly one of the matters on which we want as much information as we can get. I am not sure whether we need to refer this topic to Dr. Emminger for further study, as has been suggested; we may be able to assemble a good deal of information right here in our group.

BERNSTEIN: May I give you my answer as to what is the difference between Professor Rueff's suggestion and mine? I think Milton Gilbert has hit the point. It is the essence of Professor Rueff's approach to the problem that if you are going to undertake this major operation on the world economy in the hope that it will then recover and be very healthy, you had better make that operation once, and on a big scale—even if you have to cut out some living flesh in order to be sure that you have the cancerous growth. My suggestion is that we can offer the healing medicine in very small doses; in fact, it works best in small doses. We can keep the $14,000 bar of gold at $14,000, because we can increase the amount of Reserve Units at a regular rate. And we can make sure that this regular rate of growth is one that is suitable to the economy. We do not have to worry about whether, when you double the price of gold, the production of gold will respond twofold, or one-and-a-half-fold, or at any other figure. And we do not have to worry about how large the influx of gold will be from outside the monetary system proper—that is, from hoards and from the external countries that have gold to sell. That is what I would regard as the difference in economics between changing the price of gold and issuing Reserve Units.

TRIFFIN: I don't quite agree with that interpretation. I think there are really two problems which are mixed up here. The first is the question of gradualness. You say that we are not compelled to double the price of gold and to make a $14,000 bar of gold worth $28,000. But neither is Mr. Rueff under his plan. He does not have to double the price of gold; he can increase it by 10 per cent this year, 10 per cent next year, or at the same rate of reserve increase as under your plan. Thus the main issue, it seems to me, is not really gradualness. It is rather the difference in the distribution of reserves. Whenever you increase the price of gold, you give 100 per cent of the benefit of this operation to the gold producers and the gold holders. But if, instead of changing the price of gold, you decide to give $14,000 in Reserve Units, that $14,000 will be distributed, not according to gold holdings or gold production, but according to IMF quotas: 36 per cent will go to the United States and United Kingdom, 25 or 30 per cent will go to the less-developed countries, and 17 per cent to the EEC countries, because these are the proportions of their quotas in the Fund. This difference in distribution is at least as significant as the difference you mentioned.

BERNSTEIN: Bob, there are two separate questions that you raised. The first is whether it is a good idea to distribute reserves to countries as a matter of custom or right—whichever it may be—regardless of whether they are in deficit or in surplus. Wouldn't countries finally respond by saying: "The pattern of behavior this arrangement calls forth is intolerable; we will have to give it up"? That is Question One. Question Two is not really of great importance; it can easily be exaggerated, especially as I am myself a very flexible man. It concerns the allocation of Reserve Units on the basis of Fund quotas. The reason why the allocation figures that Mr. Triffin was able to quote turned out to be so is not because the IMF has been stubborn; it is because certain countries in the EEC group have not really wanted to have their quotas in the Fund adjusted to their position in world trade, to say nothing of world power. I would make the suggestion—which I have made in practically every paper I have written on this subject—that of course we would have to have a revision of quotas to reflect better the position of countries in world trade, and, what's more, I have always added that this would be good for the Fund. So it is not really something you could blame me for, or even the formula. To argue on the basis of the formula is really getting us off on a minor point.

TRIFFIN: I quite agree with you that the formula can be changed and that you can give 36 per cent to the EEC and 17 per cent to the United Kingdom and the United States. All I mean to say is that whatever the specific figures, the distribution seems to me to be based on a very arbitrary kind of formula. True, it is very different from the distribution resulting from a change in the price of gold, but I do not think there is much logic in either distribution.

The Group of Ten has repeatedly said that the new system should strengthen the adjustment mechanism and that there should be multilateral surveillance of all forms of reserve creation and all forms of deficit and surplus financing. Although stated very nicely three or four times in the Group's reports, all this is completely forgotten when it comes to the creation of Reserve Units; you finance deficits or you finance surpluses according to a formula which is totally independent of the adjustment mechanism and totally independent of the wisdom or folly of the policies which are being followed. If we are to distribute manna from Heaven in some form—whether it be through an increase in the price of gold, through the creation of Reserve Units, or through deposits with the IMF—I would like to distribute it in the most intelligent way possible and, in particular, in a way which strengthens the adjustment mechanism. Why should distribution be on the basis of an arbitrary formula dreamed up at Bretton Woods in 1944, or revised in 1967 by another process of logrolling, in which some countries will want increases in quotas and some countries will not?

BERNSTEIN: I will take the real heart of your point, which is that my formula for reserve distribution destroys the adjustment mechanism—and not the subsidiary question of whether manna from Heaven should be poured out to gold producers, gold hoarders, gold holders, gold speculators, or only to the monetary authorities of such countries as are prepared to create, to hold, and to use Reserve Units in reasonable amount and on reasonable terms. Let us not bother with the latter question at the moment. May we get on to the adjustment process?

RUEFF: I feel extraordinarily comforted, because I have discovered a very powerful ally in the person of Mr. Bernstein, and I am very grateful for what he said showing the link . . .

Chairman THORP: Now wait until you've heard the next thing he's going to say!

RUEFF: It is very difficult to see where we are, because there have been so many questions raised this morning. Mr. Bernstein has said that his plan would not imply giving something for nothing, because a claim is all right when there is something behind the claim. But in this case, it is purely free; it is a gift made to the country which receives the Reserve Units, and that is why, it seems to me, such a system would destroy the mechanism which tends to maintain equilibrium in the balance of payments.

May I come to a more simple question—the increase of quotas in the International Monetary Fund. It is exactly the same process. We speak with extraordinary lightheartedness of the creation of increases in Fund quotas, as if this were a purely administrative procedure. But to increase Fund quotas is to give countries a right to get real wealth in the creditor countries when they are themselves debtors. It is a way of allocating resources to the debtor country at the expense of the creditor country. Imagine the precautions which we take in all of our countries when we make public expenditures; there is the preparation of the budget, there is a control by the parliament. We have very serious needs—roads, schools, hospitals—but nevertheless we are very careful to control these expenditures. But when you increase the quotas of the Monetary Fund, you give to the debtor country the right to take wealth from the creditor country without any sacrifice and without any control of any kind outside the Fund itself.

When Mr. Bernstein speaks of a "claim," if I understand correctly, it is the same thing. It is quite different from a claim which results from the production of goods—of wheat, of steel; it is more or less the same as the treasury bill in a deficit country, without any real counterpart behind it. Am I right?

TRIFFIN: I would like to add to your statement, because it illuminates another point which Mr. Bernstein touched on a minute ago. You say that when there is an increase in Fund quotas, it means that countries will be able to borrow more. If this were the only effect, I think that every country would like to get as large a quota as possible. But we find that, as Mr. Bernstein indicated, some countries do not want to have their quotas increased. Other countries do. This is because an increase in quota may have two totally opposite implications, depending on your expectations—which may be wrong—about your future balance of payments. If you expect to be a debtor, it means a *right to borrow* more. If you expect to be a creditor, it means an *obligation to lend* more. In either case, this carries the same amount of voting right in the Fund—that is to say, you reward with the same amount of voting right an obligation to lend and a right to borrow. And this is one of the crucial problems which our friends in the Group of Ten have to contend with—the question of voting rights in the new system. I must say that there is a very big difference in this respect between my proposal and Bretton Woods, or the proposal of Mr. Bernstein; it is that I do not propose to expand the international credit base through increases in quotas. The deposits in the Fund which I have suggested have nothing to do with any kind of logrolling about how large each quota will be; they will develop in accordance with the balances of payments, and in a very different way.

BERNSTEIN: I must say that this, in my view, is the worst system—that the growth of reserves should develop according to the amount of imbalance or deficits in international payments. But I think this all comes back to the problem of whether a system of creating credit reserves or, indeed, reserves in any form but gold, is consistent with the maintenance of balance-of-payments discipline. I am convinced myself that the system I propose *is* consistent with balance-of-payments discipline. I will not say that Mr. Triffin's approach is inconsistent with such discipline, but, in the first instance, it makes the creation of reserves an accident of there being balance-of-payments deficits.

TRIFFIN: No . . .

BERNSTEIN: Well, just one second, Bob. This all depends on whether we take Triffin I or Triffin II.

TRIFFIN: No; what I wrote in 1959 is the same as what I said in 1966 on that issue.

BERNSTEIN: We shall soon see. After I have explained myself, Mr. Triffin can show how I have misinterpreted his views of 1959 or 1966. Let us suppose that a country has a balance-of-payments deficit. It comes to the Triffin Central Bank and gets a credit. The reserves of the world are increased by the amount of that credit. Now suppose the world has a very prosperous period, in which prices of basic commodities are reasonably stable, in which the big countries are not inflating—or at least not inflating at different rates—and we are in a rare period of a well-balanced pattern of payments. Nobody comes to the Triffin Bank to borrow. So, in this period, there is no increase in reserves through the extension of Triffin credits. I do not know what I have missed here on the lending side of the system. What have I misinterpreted, Bob?

TRIFFIN: It is very simple; I said both in Triffin I and in Triffin II . . .

BERNSTEIN: May I add one last sentence? Suppose that a country which previously borrowed from the Triffin Bank now has a good balance of payments and repays; then the reserves of the world have gone down. What about this?

TRIFFIN: What I wrote in 1959 and in 1966 on this matter

is exactly the same thing. I said that the over-all creation of world reserves should not depend on the pattern of deficits or lending; I said that the Fund should attempt to guide the over-all growth of reserves in such a way as to combat inflationary or deflationary pressures in the world economy. Its actual lending should be larger in a period of deflationary pressure and smaller in a period of inflation. I said, however—and I am very glad to see that I am here in full agreement with the way Dr. Emminger expressed himself in his last report—that this would lead in all likelihood to some sort of presumptive target criterion. Normally, you would expect that the growth of world reserves as a whole should keep some kind of relation to the growth of trade and production—perhaps something on the order of 4 to 6 per cent a year. To the extent that this reserve increase is provided by gold, all right, but since, according to recent experience, gold would provide maybe 1 per cent growth a year instead of 4 to 6 per cent, the total lending of the Fund should make up the difference. I think that I accept completely the formulation of the last Group of Ten Report, and I do not think it differs in any way from my position in 1959 or in 1966.

BERNSTEIN: But suppose there are no deficits; how do you lend the money?

TRIFFIN: I am not terribly worried about the problem of nobody wanting to borrow. That seems to me a rather unlikely occurrence, but if it happened it would surely mean that reserves were adequate. I would not be worried at all if, during one year or two years, the Fund did no lending at all because no country felt that its reserves were inadequate. In any case, there would still be a possibility of increasing reserves in the Triffin Plan both of 1959 and of 1966. I said in 1959 that if the Fund is to lend these fairly substantial amounts year after year, it should not confine itself to what I call advances, or drawings if you like, but should use a new technique—namely, investment. I suggested that part of the investment might be made in bonds of the IBRD, and I said also that it could be made in the large financial markets, which would help those markets to play their role in overseas lending. This is exactly what the Fund itself proposed in 1964 in its annual report. The report stated that the Fund, at its own discretion, and not at the request of any particular member, would engage in a certain amount of investment with the purpose of guiding the over-all evolution of world reserves. Under such a policy, the Fund might lend, let us say, $1 billion or $2 billion a year, and then would decide to whom to lend and in what form, whether through investment or drawings.

There is one matter, however, in which I recognize that Dr. Bernstein has a very good point: If loans were to be regularly repaid after three to five years, as in the present Fund arrangements, the Fund would soon have to do an enormous amount of new lending in order both to offset the repayments and to provide, in spite of these repayments, the desired increase in world reserves. It is just in this connection that the investment technique would be especially useful, because such investment can be of a longer-term character. Several years ago, the Fund invested several hundred million dollars in U.S. Treasury bills. This loan to the United States was not repaid after three years or five years. In fact, it may never be repaid. As long as the Fund considers this a proper investment, it is not compelled to undo that investment. So there really is no problem of obtaining the desired increase in world reserves under the Triffin Plan either of 1959 or of 1966.

Chairman THORP: The Chairman must intervene at this point, since we have just reached an extraordinary position of balance: each speaker has spoken exactly the same number of words. As all good things must end, the only fair procedure is to adjourn now.

CHAPTER VIII

THE GOLD-EXCHANGE STANDARD AND
THE PRICE OF GOLD

I have taken the floor only because the Group of Ten has been criticized, although I must say it was very mild criticism (I am accustomed to much more severe criticism of our work), and because there have been a number of appeals to our group to take up certain questions. Professor Rueff, in particular, seems to have an exaggerated notion of our capabilities. He relies upon us to contribute substantially to the solution of such enormously difficult questions as how to improve the policies for adjusting to balance-of-payments deficits. He appeals to us to study past experiences of adjustment during the gold standard period. He also asks us to study the flexibility of gold production in relation to prices. I may have overlooked some other appeals, but I have taken notes and, when I return home, I will try to attend to all these matters.

I

I first want to say one thing about the *diagnosis* of the present situation, because here I am happy to report very complete agreement with what has been said at this conference. The Group of Ten has not proceeded from the assumption, as is very often incorrectly said in newspaper reports, that there is a shortage of liquidity. Perhaps, therefore, Professor Rueff's analogy to the Gold Committee of the League of Nations is not entirely correct. On the contrary, in our last report we concluded that, at the present time,

* One of Europe's ablest and best-known central bankers, Otmar Emminger has been a member of the Board of Governors of the German central bank since 1953. He has served as an executive director of the International Monetary Fund and as vice-president of the Monetary Committee of the European Economic Community. As chairman of the Deputies of the Group of Ten, he occupies a central position in official thinking and negotiations on international monetary reform.

there is no shortage of liquidity. But, on the other hand, we also concluded that there is at least a likelihood that, at some point in the future, the traditional sources of reserves—namely, gold and dollars—will not be adequate for the needs of the world. This working assumption is based on two further assumptions: first, that the price of gold will not be raised (on this, I have to say a few words later) and that therefore we will have to rely on the foreseeable volume of new gold coming into the monetary orbit on the basis of the present gold price; and secondly—this is quite an important assumption—that the deficit in the U.S. balance of payments cannot continue indefinitely and that the possibilities for financing this deficit just by dollar accumulation with foreign central banks have nearly reached, or may have already reached, their limit, so that the gold-exchange standard as a source of new reserves is for all practical purposes out. And we have also said, with the full concurrence of the American members of our group, that we would even regret any further large-scale increase of external short-term indebtedness of the United States. So the gold-exchange standard in the future, at least in our opinion, will no longer be a source of any sizable amount of new reserves.

II

I would now like to say a few words about the general problem of adjustment policies in deficit situations. Here I come back to Professor Rueff's suggestion that the Group of Ten should go into this. As a matter of fact, as some of you probably know, we have gone into this question, though not in our capacity as Deputies of the Group of Ten. With a mandate from the Group of Ten, and for the purpose of division of labor, because the Group of Ten itself was overburdened with work, we—that is, essentially the same people—looked into this matter in our capacity as members of the OECD. We studied the problem for one and a half years and published our first report in late 1966.

Some people have said it was a good report. I personally would not consider it a very satisfying report, because it showed very clearly that a modern government is very wary of any firm commitments concerning its balance-of-payments policies. The reluctance to undertake firm commitments is especially noticeable in the case of the Anglo-Saxon countries. Both the United Kingdom and the United States have been very reluctant to go along with such "rules of the game," at least where these rules amount to commitments. Of course we, and especially I—coming from a central bank—are imbued with the notion that whenever you have a deficit in your balance of payments, there should be a primary effect on your monetary base at home, and thus on your aggregate demand; but we have found that in some countries this automatic primary deflationary effect does not exist, because the machinery works in such a way that it counteracts this first automatic adjustment. I refer in this connection particularly to Great Britain, with its Exchange Equalization Fund.

Another question that may be asked, and which to some extent we have already put to ourselves, is whether we could expect any increase in this automatic adjustment pressure if, as Professor Rueff proposes, we were to abolish the gold-exchange standard. We have come to the conclusion—it was implicit in the report—that irrespective of whether a country loses gold or foreign exchange, there will be the same primary automatic effect; but that countries, in certain circumstances, will take measures to counteract this automatic effect, at least to some extent, regardless of whether we have a gold standard or a gold-exchange standard. Even under a pure gold standard—and this has been mentioned already by Professor Rueff—governments and central banks can still counteract these automatic effects. So, even under a pure gold standard, there is no guarantee that the adjustment to external imbalance will work better, because everything depends on whether governments really agree voluntarily to commit themselves to the rules of the game. In trying to agree on rules for the "adjustment process" between the members of the Group of Ten, we saw how far one can get today in the effort to make sovereign, independent states commit themselves to such rules. I would repeat that what you can expect is rather limited; and there would be no change in this limitation on commitments even if we were to move to a pure gold reserve standard.

This leads me to a further point. We have seen that the gold-exchange standard may have had inflationary effects in the past, as described by Professor Rueff. There was hardly any difference of opinion on that. But we have also seen that, in the recent past, there has no longer been any such effect and that it is unlikely that there will be such an effect, to any important extent, in the future.

Let me explain that by concrete examples. The first concerns Great Britain, which is one of the reserve currency countries. There has been practically no increase in the sterling balances officially held abroad by Sterling Area countries for a great number of years; there has been some increase in other balances held in connection with assistance operations, but not as sterling reserves. Thus the fact that countries hold sterling as official reserves has been of no help to Great Britain in balancing its external accounts. On the contrary, whenever the United Kingdom has encountered balance-of-payments difficulties, it has felt added pressure from that source, because sterling was converted into dollars or gold. So the gold-exchange standard in the case of Britain has, for a number of years, worked in the direction of adding pressure to the country—and not of giving it more leeway to run deficits.

For the United States, the situation is perhaps a little different, but even there we have recently seen a similar change in the working of the gold-exchange standard. From the end of 1964 to the end of September, 1966 (the latest figure I have with me), the official dollar holdings of foreign central banks—including special forms of claims against the United States like Roosa bonds, which are just dollar holdings with an exchange guarantee attached to them— have decreased by about $1 billion. Now this means, of course, that since 1964 the United States has no longer had any help from the gold-exchange standard; on the contrary, during this period, the United States has had to cover its entire deficit, and even more than the deficit, by drawing on its gold reserves and IMF position. In other words, so far as the unsound or unwelcome or undesirable effects are concerned, the gold-exchange standard for all practical purposes has been dead since 1964. Nevertheless—and this is most significant—the fact that the United States has been since the end of 1964, in effect, no longer on a gold-exchange standard but on a pure gold standard has not had any perceptible impact on the balance-of-payments adjustment policies of that country. This must give us some food for thought regarding the alleged balance-of-payments discipline entailed by being on a pure gold standard. Unfortunately, I must draw the conclusion that we would need more than just a return to the pure gold standard in order to improve balance-of-payments performance in this world.

III

Now I must say a few words on the price of gold. As I indicated earlier, the Group of Ten has been basing its work and its conclusions on the assumption that the price of gold will not be changed. As Deputies, we have complied with our instructions in this matter, but nobody has said to us that we were forbidden to think about the assumption—and we have thought about it. As early as two and a half years ago, we circulated an internal memorandum on this question and we have also taken account of the new arguments that have come up in the meantime. I will tell you why it is likely that we will continue to base our thinking on the assumption that there will be no change in the price of gold.

As I see the situation, there are three major reasons for arguing that the present price should be changed. One reason is closely related to what I have just discussed, the working of the gold-exchange standard. Professor Rueff wants an increase in the price of gold in order to enable the United States to repay the outstanding dollar balances held by foreign central banks. He even said, in an interview which attracted wide attention, that an increase in the price of gold would make sense to him only if it were used to repay the outstanding dollar balances.

We are not so certain that such a repayment is absolutely necessary, or that it is even possible or practicable to repay all the outstanding official dollar holdings. We are rather of the opinion that it would be quite sufficient if the level of dollar balances remained more or less where it is and did not show any large-scale increase. We do not look so much to the past; we look to the future, and what we want is that there not be any further lax policies based on the gold-exchange standard. In our view, the expansionary phase of the gold-exchange standard is a chapter that we have concluded; and we do not want to have any further substantial piling up of official dollar holdings.

But we want to go a little further, not by means of a firm

legal commitment but by what we call a "multilateral surveillance"—one of those funny newfangled expressions—
among the major countries. You cannot, of course, police the
105 member countries of the Fund, but you can to some
extent police yourself in a smaller group of countries, and,
within such a group, you can also reach some understanding
about reserve policies. One of the major understandings
about these reserve policies should be that the level of dollar
reserves should not rise very greatly above the present level.
As I have said, this has already been more or less achieved
in the recent past. Thus, in our opinion, there is no need for
an increase in the price of gold in order to repay the outstanding dollar balances, because we would just regard that
as a thing of the past. This past accumulation of dollar
balances was not a sin; it made very good sense in some
ways, but I would repeat that it is a chapter of the past and
that our concern now should be to prevent any unsound
practices in the future.

A second argument for an increase in the price of gold is
the notion that this price is out of any proper relationship
with other prices, because, since 1934, it has remained
stationary at $35 per ounce while commodity prices have
more or less doubled. Here again I must say that I am not
very much impressed by this argument for a number of
reasons which I will enumerate very briefly.

First, who really knows whether the relationship established in 1934 was the proper and correct relationship,
which therefore has to be restored now and kept ever after?
In 1934 we had a very arbitrary increase in the price of
gold by 69 per cent. Why was the relationship proper then?
Nobody can answer that question. But my argument goes a
little further. I doubt whether it is a good philosophy to
argue that the price of gold should from time to time, even
if only very rarely, be adjusted to the movement of prices in
the world. Doesn't this really go directly against the very
idea of utilizing gold as a fixed reference point? I quote
General de Gaulle, who said in his famous press conference
of February, 1965, that "gold should be and is the immuta-
ble and fiduciary value par excellence." Now if we adhere to
the philosophy that the price of gold should be adjusted
every ten or every fifteen years—whatever you like—to the
movement of other prices, I think we would be making the

price of gold merely an index of the propensity of governments to inflate. I would hate to put gold into such a relative position, no longer to be taken as a firm anchor or firm base. This does not mean that we should not study the price of gold for other reasons, such as production or private demand, but these other reasons are less compelling, and if anything comes out of such an examination, there are a number of ways of dealing with it.

A further point which makes me skeptical about an increase in the price of gold is the question of the United States. There has been some talk about whether there is a legal or moral commitment on the part of the United States to maintain the present gold value of the dollar. Of course there is no *legal* commitment; there is, however, what has been explicitly called by several presidents of the United States a "pledge"—that was the word used by President Kennedy— or a "commitment"—the word used by President Johnson—to maintain the present gold value of the dollar; and it is on the basis of this pledge or commitment that a number of central banks have held their dollars instead of converting them into gold. There are no other agreements about the convertibility of the dollar into gold at the present price except this pledge, supported by the self-interest, in an enlightened sense, of the whole monetary system. This commitment, then, is something that the United States cannot abandon lightly.

But let us leave aside the pledge. Let us leave aside the moral aspect—it is not moral; it is really a financial pledge, which is something else than moral. But let's leave all that aside. I wonder what would happen if a negotiation about a new gold price were to begin. Professor Rueff feels—and this is quite proper—that a new gold price should not be set just by the United States at its own discretion but should come about by common agreement. This is proper, because the matter affects all other countries very deeply. But how would such an agreement be worked out? Of course, you cannot negotiate without telling other people what you are about to do, and I wonder whether there is any moral obligation on the part of the more than a hundred central banks in the world to refrain from converting their dollars into gold at the present price, once they are alerted that this price is soon to be changed.

It is no use pretending that we could have normal negotiations if these negotiations were conducted in a very secret way. You know that in modern democracies it is very difficult to keep anything of that sort secret. There would be continuous suspicion that something is happening. I personally do not see very much possibility for establishing a new gold price except through a temporary suspension of the sale of gold by the United States and the suspension of the London gold market by the countries of the Gold Pool—since, if any rumors were to get out, the market would go through the roof. Of course, this would appear to all the outside countries to be a one-sided act decided upon by the United States, because it could inform its partners only after it had suspended gold sales.

Moreover, it is quite clear that the amount of any such increase in the gold price would not be decided upon in what we call the "ordinary" procedure for creating reserves—that is to say, by voting upon new reserves. We in the Group of Ten have devoted a great deal of time to this problem, because the question of who is going to control the creation of international reserves is a basic political question. Practically speaking, the decision in this case would have to be made by the United States alone, because in the end the whole new system would depend on the readiness of the United States to accept the new gold price. I think this consideration makes it very difficult to conceive of a rise in the gold price coming about in a very orderly way, though I would entirely agree with Professor Rueff that it would be of the greatest importance to take such action in an orderly way and without a crisis. But it would not be easy.

Now I don't want to go into many more points, but let me say just one thing about the inflationary aspects of an increase in the price of gold. I must say that I am deeply worried by what is being said on this subject. We in the Group of Ten have never talked officially about any specific magnitude of new reserves to be created in the future, but we have on occasion used some illustrative figures. I remember such an illustrative figure that found its way, some time ago, into the American newspapers—the usual leak, because one cannot keep anything secret nowadays. It did not do any harm, even though the figure cited, an annual creation of $2 billion, was wrong—the illustrative figure actually used was

different. But I remember what an outcry there was in some
conservative Continental European circles and among some
central bankers that anybody would be so inflation-minded
as to consider the artificial creation of reserves to the tune
of $2 billion.

Now, this morning I have heard talk of a doubling of the
price of gold. This would mean, even after repayment of
part of the foreign exchange reserves, the creation of from
$17 billion up to $41 billion—all in one stroke! To this would
be added the inflationary effects of several billion dollars of
gold dishoarding.

I must say I was terrified. Of course you may say that by
sterilizing the book profits on the revalued gold reserves,
you can sterilize a large part of the inflationary effects of a
rise in the gold price. But what you do with the domestic
money which arises from the book profit is only part of the
problem. With some effort, you can sterilize it if you can
control spendthrift parliaments and governments, but what
you will not have compensated for is the effect of the greatly
increased *external* liquidity, which is still there—the increase in reserves which enables all countries to pursue
much more expansionary policies than would otherwise be
possible. And, in this connection, there is no comfort to be
derived from the proposal to lend some part of these reserves to other countries. Lending part of the reserves to
countries like the United Kingdom or the underdeveloped
countries would make expansionary policies even more
likely.

Finally, there is, of course, the political problem of
distribution or allocation. We must not forget that an increase in the price of gold which suddenly increases the
book value of existing gold stocks is just as much a distribution of reserves, or "manna from Heaven," as the allocation
of Reserve Units along the lines of the Bernstein model
would be. In fact, increasing the value of gold stocks at the
stroke of a pen is the only method of creating and dis-
tributing reserves *ex nihilo*. All other methods (for example, the deliberate creation of Reserve Units) involve an
exchange of mutual drawing rights—that is, a *quid pro quo*.
With an increase in the gold price, we have to look very
carefully into the formula according to which this manna
from Heaven would be distributed. I am not so much con-

cerned with the benefits to the gold-producing countries—
Russia, South Africa, and so on—though they would of
course be large. To some extent I would share Lord Robbins'
opinion on that. But I am concerned with the distribution of
benefits to those who hold gold; and here I must say that we
would be confronted with the most unjust, the most
arbitrary, distribution one could think of. Eighty-five per
cent of the new reserves created would go to the countries of
the Group of Ten, as they hold that proportion of total gold
reserves. Countries that have relied on the U.S. pledge and
have held a lower gold proportion in their reserves would
be penalized. Gold hoarders would be rewarded.

It is no consolation to say that part of the benefits would
be redistributed in loans. In the first place, I think it would
be extremely difficult to agree on these loans. In the second
place, for underdeveloped, poor countries it would be no
comfort to get on a loan basis, with a gold value attached,
what others get, not as a loan but as a gift. The rich countries would get gifts—including the United States, which
would wipe out its dollar debt to central banks. The non-
gold-holding countries would get nothing but the very feeble
prospect of gold-guaranteed loans. We have had the experience of being confronted with the views of 105 countries
in joint meetings between the Group of Ten and the Executive Directors of the Fund. I can tell you that we have
had a much better proposal for allocating newly created
reserves, but even that has been severely criticized. So, politically speaking, it would be extremely difficult to sell such
an arbitrary distribution scheme to the world.

My feeling therefore is that in the light of all these
difficulties of orderly transition, of distribution, and of inflationary potential, an increase in the price of gold is not an
acceptable solution. In our view, we do not need a change in
the gold price, as we are convinced that there are other and
better ways of providing for legitimate international reserve needs.

What would happen if, following a big crisis, the present
price of gold could no longer be maintained? I am very
doubtful whether the United States would then immediately
say, "Well now, we are coming around from our old position
and will joyfully agree to a 50 per cent or a 100 per cent
increase in the price of gold!" What would happen would

very likely be something different. There would be a return to the slogan of "going it alone"; the gold window at the U.S. Treasury would be shut, not just for a few months but for a few years, until we were under a new system which, I can assure you, would be quite different from the old. But that might take some years, and in the meantime we would quite certainly not be on a gold standard but on a dollar standard, and the world payments system and world trade might be subjected to some disagreeable jolts.

All these considerations, I must say, have made me very cautious in dealing with the problem of the gold price. That is why I so much regret that this very delicate problem, which can of course be easily discussed in a circle such as this, has now been taken up in the public market place by some governments. I do not believe that this will really give us a very good or rational solution. But, on the other hand, I am now convinced that it is our duty to work more quickly than we have until now. We have not worked very fast in the Group of Ten on a new system, since we all had the feeling that there was no great urgency. Now, however, I have come to the conclusion that events may drive us to the point where we will have to come out rather quickly with a good, rational solution to the international reserve problem.

William J. Busschau, Donald H. McLaughlin,
Michael Spieler*

THE PRICE OF GOLD AND
THE LEVEL OF WORLD GOLD RESERVES

A special feature of the Bologna Center conference was the attention paid to factual questions regarding gold and the price of gold. Among the participants were three internationally recognized authorities on gold—William J. Busschau, Donald H. McLaughlin, and Michael Spieler—and advantage was taken of their presence to explore the probable effect of an increase in price on production and on dishoarding and, therefore, on the level of world gold reserves. The impact on industrial consumption, for which allowance would also have to be made in predicting the effect of a price increase on world gold reserves, was not explored at the conference. In a letter to the editor, however, Mr. Spieler has since expressed his own view that the "industrial demand for gold is rather inelastic and that, for many uses, an increase in the price would not diminish the demand because of the technical superiority of gold." Clearly, this is a subject on which further enlightenment would be helpful.

Since Jacques Rueff had proposed that the price of gold be "approximately doubled," the three experts were asked to base their thinking on the assumption of a $70 price per ounce. As they would be the first to insist, their estimates

---

* Generally recognized as one of the world's leading gold experts, William J. Busschau is Chancellor of Rhodes University. He is the author of *The Measure of Gold* and other works.

A leading figure in American mining, Donald H. McLaughlin taught at Harvard and at the University of California, Berkeley, where he was dean of the College of Mining and later dean of the College of Engineering. He has long served as a Regent of the University of California, and in 1958–60 was chairman of the Board of Regents. He is chairman of the board of the Homestake Mining Company.

A leading expert on gold, Michael Spieler is financial adviser to the Union Corporation, Ltd., London.

inevitably are highly conjectural. Nor are they in complete agreement; with respect to dishoarding, it will be noted that Mr. Spieler arrives at a conclusion somewhat different from that of Dr. Busschau. Nevertheless, the estimates are of great interest as a reflection of the most expert opinion.

The statements that follow are presented in the order in which they were made. Each statement was revised by its author after the conference to take account of more recent figures than were available at the time of the meeting.

R. H.

THE GOLD PRICE AND U.S. GOLD OUTPUT

Donald H. McLaughlin

My remarks will be brief, as the United States is a relatively small gold producer. For example, out of a total world output of $1.4 billion in 1965, the United States produced $59 million, or a little over 4 per cent.

Grade of ore, nature and size of the deposit, depth in the earth, location, and a number of other geological and technical considerations determine the cost of producing gold. When costs catch up with the value of the output, a mine closes. This may happen even when large tonnages of material below the grade necessary for profits are still available. When wages and the purchase of equipment and supplies must be met in a depreciating currency that forces higher costs in every category, and when the gold must be sold at the price fixed by governmental authority, profits obviously decline and national production falls, except as it may be offset by new discoveries of exceptional sort and by technical improvements, which are hard to achieve in an already efficiently managed and experienced industry.

Under these conditions, gold production throughout the world has declined over the past twenty-five years, except in South Africa. There, the discovery of a new and richer gold field in the Orange Free State and the development of new mines under deep cover along extensions of the known reefs of the Witwatersrand, as well as profits from uranium that have prolonged the lives of a number of marginal mines, resulted in a substantial increase in output of gold that more than offset the decline elsewhere.

Without this fortunate occurrence, the crisis in gold would have been upon us much sooner. However, with the flattening of the rate of production in South Africa which is

already apparent, and with the increased demand for gold
for nonmonetary purposes, the time is now very near when
far-reaching decisions must be made. Either an acceptable
substitute for gold as money will have to be found which
will drastically reduce the quantity of gold needed for the
world's monetary reserves, or gold will have to be revalued
to a level that will offset the depreciation that the dollar and
other currencies have suffered since 1940.

If the price of gold were to be doubled, the gold-mining
industry would be in the same position as in 1940, since the
price level of other commodities has doubled since then. The
immediate effect would probably be a temporary decline in
annual output measured in ounces, for existing mill capacity
would be used for lower-grade ores that would then become
profitable. Within a few years, however—say, three to five
years—the great stimulus to exploration and to the building
of new plants would result in increased production. With
good fortune, the output of the late 1930s might be restored
in the United States, Canada, and Australia, but this would
require the discovery of new districts to replace a number of
major districts that would be difficult to revive.

If the present price of gold remains in effect, the U.S. gold
industry is going to decline substantially very soon. One
strange effect right now is that, for an existing mine to stay
in business, it has to increase its rate of output to restrain
the rise in unit costs. Thus, the output of gold may be temporarily increased, but at the cost of shortening the life of
the mine. One gets an ominous sense of doom as precious
reserves are dissipated with declining profits while the cost
curve continues to approach the flat ceiling of revenues
imposed by the fixed price of gold.

According to the trend line of a few years ago, we would
be out of business now. Of course, there have been many
technical improvements in this industrial age that have flat-
tened the curve. But the curve still goes up. I hate to say
this, but I think that with no change in the price of gold the
Homestake Mine, which is operated by the company of
which I am chairman and which is the largest gold mine in
the free world outside South Africa, will be out of business
within three to five years even though the ore body is still
far from being exhausted. This would mean that a third of
current U.S. production would close down.

There may, of course, be new discoveries. In recent years,

there was an excellent new mine developed by the Newmont Company—an open-pit operation with a metallurgically difficult ore. It was found by bold and well directed development undertaken by the Newmont Company, guided by some excellent work of the U.S. Geological Survey. We were following the same idea, but Newmont happened to get to the right place first. But this is a rather small thing. It would take several discoveries of this magnitude to offset the decline that soon must be expected elsewhere.

Thus, if the present price is maintained, I foresee a drop in the U.S. production of gold in the early 1970s to the quantity recovered as a by-product from the base metal mines (principally the porphyry coppers) supplemented possibly from another open-pit mine or two, amounting to a reduction to about 1.1 million ounces from the present annual output of 1.8 million ounces. But U.S. output is so small in relation to world gold production that I think I should stop and let Dr. Busschau carry on for the Free World as a whole.

The Gold Price, Gold Output, and Gold Hoarding

William J. Busschau

I have been asked to make some estimates of the future world production of gold, both on the assumption that the gold price is maintained at its present level of $35 an ounce and on the alternative assumption that the price is raised to $70. The first thing I should say is that, whatever the price of gold, production would not be much affected over the next three years because of the lag that Dr. McLaughlin has talked about.

But let me begin with the $35 price. On the basis of information from large numbers of companies, the peak in free world gold production would be at about the level reached this past year—that is, about 42 million ounces. Now convert this figure into dollars, if you wish, and you get about $1.5 billion.

To look into the future, I shall have to do some projecting, which is not very sensible because human ingenuity is at work. New fields may be discovered. Another possibility is an increased use of uranium, which would involve increased output of gold as a joint product. I think we can conclude that uranium is still used on a very small scale. Human ingenuity will no doubt expand its uses. To mention only one matter, taking the salt out of sea water might create an enormous demand for uranium, and that could mean additional gold production from sources that would not at present be worked for their gold content but that at even $35 an ounce could be worked for the joint products of uranium and gold.

But if one ignores these highly conjectural possibilities, which in any case are of a longer-run character, I would on these restrictive assumptions guess that by 1970, at the $35 price, the annual gold output would be, say, $1.45 billion. It would then fall rather rapidly. By 1980 it would be below $1 billion and by 1987 it would be in the neighborhood of, say, $500 million. I can project the figure further, but I think that in human affairs it is not sensible to try to look too far ahead.

It is sometimes concluded that if you double the price of gold, you get an enormous increase in production. Of course, if you change the price, then you change the money value of the increment. But in terms of ounces, whether the price is $52.50 or $70 does not make much difference over the first three years, because the immediate effect of a higher price would be to mine lower-grade material. Assuming that the price were to be raised *now* to $70, my estimate of world gold output for 1970 would be about $3.0 billion (my estimate at the $35 price, you will recall, was $1.45 billion). Thus I have assumed that the physical volume of production in 1970 is about the same at either price. In my estimates at the $70 price for the years after 1970, I have made some allowance for increases in cost resulting from digging deeper in some mines, but I have assumed that increased efficiency would balance any other small increases in cost. I have also assumed no fresh discoveries, which in fact there would be, as the higher price would give an impetus to exploration. But overlooking this possibility, my figure of $3.0 billion for 1970 would fall very gradually, so that by 1980 it might be, say, $2.8 billion. This is very different from the trend in physical production if the price stays at $35. In other words, at the $70 price, the curve, instead of falling rapidly, goes at once to a higher plane, straightens out, and stays up much longer.

If you wish, I can give you the figures in ounces. At the $35 price, my figure for 1970 is just about 41 million ounces. By 1975 it falls to 36 million ounces and, by 1980, to about 27 million ounces. If the price were increased to $70 now, my figure on the "restrictive assumptions" for 1970 would be slightly higher than that at the $35 price—that is, about 43 million ounces. By 1975 it would be about the same and, by 1980, fall to something like 41 million ounces.

It is desirable, however, to make a more realistic guess, and to allow for the revival of defunct mines, for production from freshly discovered properties, and for additional production from mines capable of producing gold and uranium jointly. On this "realistic" basis it would appear that production by 1970 should at $70 per ounce be in the order of 47 million ounces ($3.3 billion), and that from 1975 to 1980 production should in the order of 50 million ounces ($3.5 billion). In other words, if out of this private users and holders took their traditional one-third, there would still be enough left for official holders to feed their reserves adequately.

Now I should say a few words about hoarding, as this very much affects the level of world monetary reserves. Historically, about a third of all mined gold has been hoarded in some sense. I do not like the word "hoarding," because holders of gold hold it for various reasons; in some countries, they hold it for monetary purposes. And I believe it is very difficult, in fact, to distinguish the reasons, as some people have more freedom to hold gold than others. Americans are prohibited from holding gold, as well as Britons and, for the time being, we South Africans. But in the Middle East one can hold gold, and gold can have a monetary use. I would therefore prefer to talk about "personal" and "official" holdings of gold.

The question of how much out of the existing "personal holdings" would find its way into official reserves after a rise in the price of gold is a very difficult one. I do not think that we can learn much from the experience of the 1930's. You have to remember that there was a catastrophic fall in agricultural prices and that what we now call the developing countries were in great difficulties. The rise in the gold price at that time led to a great deal of dishoarding because, in a sense, the Indians and others had to eat their gold. The situa-

tion now, of course, is very different, and the rise in the gold
price would probably have to be very great to induce a sizable
release from hoards. If you ask me to guess what would happen at a price of $70, I would say that I do not think the dis-
hoarding would amount to more than 150 million ounces,
which in my opinion would be a great relief to the monetary
authorities holding foreign currencies as if they were proper
substitutes for gold reserves.

THE GOLD PRICE AND GOLD DISHOARDING

Michael Spieler

Since the end of World War II, the gold production of the
Western world, including Russian gold sales to the West,
has totaled approximately 732 million ounces, or $25.6 bil-
lion at the present price. These gold supplies have been
absorbed in approximately the following way:

WORLD GOLD DISTRIBUTION, 1946–66
(millions of ounces)

1. To official monetary reserves	290 (40%)
2. To industry, jewelry, and the arts	156 (21%)
3. To traditional hoarding centers	173 (24%)
4. To other private gold holders	113 (15%)
	732

The proportion of the new gold supply that has been absorbed by the traditional hoarding centers and other private
holders has increased significantly in recent years. Together
they absorbed about two-thirds of the new gold supply in
1966, a year in which no gold was added to official monetary
reserves. The changing pattern of world gold distribution
during the period 1946–66 is illustrated in Table IX-1.

I have been given the difficult assignment of attempting
to estimate the amount of gold that would be dishoarded if
the gold price were to raised to, say, $70 per ounce. I should
first, however, provide some background.

Gold hoarding is based partly on deeply rooted psychological attitudes, in areas of the world such as the Middle East,
India, and the Far East, where savings are traditionally
held in the form of gold, and partly on fears concerning the
value and stability of paper money in the more sophisticated
economies. Accordingly, it is impossible to predict or esti-

Table IX–1
WORLD GOLD SUPPLY AND DISTRIBUTION, 1946–66
(millions of ounces)

	1946–55		1956–66		1966		Total (1946–66)	
Supply:								
Production (excluding U.S.S.R.):	241.1		350.2		41.7		633.0	
Sales by U.S.S.R. to rest of world:	8.0		90.8		nil		98.8	
Total new supply:	249.1		441.0		41.7		731.8	
Distribution:		(%)		(%)		(%)		(%)
To official monetary reserves:	123.1	49.4	167.0	37.0	nil	nil	290.1	39.6
To industry, jewelry, and arts:	55.1	22.1	86.3	19.6	14.5	34.8	155.9	21.3
To traditional hoarding centers (net):	70.9	28.5	86.9	19.7	15.0	36.0	172.8	23.6
Other private holdings:			100.8	22.8	12.2	29.2	113.0	15.5
Total distribution:	249.1	100.0	441.0	100.0	41.7	100.0	731.8	100.0

This analysis is based on gold production and distribution figures published annually by Union Corporation Limited.

mate with any accuracy the reaction of gold hoarders to any particular event, since such a prediction involves an assumption about the future political and economic climate. Nevertheless, it may be useful to calculate how much gold could flow into official monetary reserves if certain assumptions are made about the behavior of the different groups of private gold hoarders.

At the outset, we should examine the words "hoarding" and "dishoarding" in this context. It has been customary in the past to apply the label "hoarding" to gold that has neither flowed into official monetary reserves nor been used in industry, dentistry, or for artistic and jewelry purposes, but has been absorbed by private individuals and institutions as a means of holding savings and as a store of value. Most of this gold has gone to the "traditional hoarding centers" (see Table IX-1)—namely, the Middle East, India, the Far East, and France.

In recent years, however, a significant part of each year's gold supply has gone neither to official monetary reserves nor to industry and the arts, nor could it be traced to the traditional hoarding centers. This gold has been purchased by individuals and institutions—for example, by the oil sheikdoms—and possibly even by some central banks of countries that are not bound by the IMF rules. It has been held in banks and safe deposits in Switzerland and elsewhere, partly as a protection against currency depreciation or against restrictions on remittances in times of monetary disturbance or political upheaval (See "other private gold holders" in Table IX-1).

In practice there is some overlapping among the different types of gold consumption. For example, in India it is usual for peasants to keep their gold savings in the form of simple jewelry. Similarly, gold is being sold by the official authorities in Saigon today, at a rate of approximately 1 million ounces a year, as a means of combatting inflation. The government of South Vietnam sells it to fabricators, who turn it into small strips. These are then sold to "jewelry" firms that sell two sizes of gold pieces to the public, one size at $50 and the other at $100. Obviously, this kind of gold absorption could be described as jewelry sales, as traditional hoarding, or even as a form of monetary demand.

Following the adjustment of currency values in the early 1930s, it appears that dishoarding by the traditional gold hoarding centers amounted to more than 80 per cent of the gold absorbed into those same hoards after World War I. With the higher price of gold, there was also some dishoarding by industry, jewelry, and the arts, which on balance released into official monetary reserves 10 to 15 per cent of the gold they had absorbed after World War I.

It does not follow, of course, that the dishoarding experience of the 1930s will have any relevance to today's circumstances in the event of a doubled gold price. There were special reasons for the massive gold dishoarding of the 1930s, such as the forced liquidation during the depression years of savings held in gold and the ban on private gold holdings imposed by the United Kingdom and the United States. Nevertheless, a doubling of the gold price would undoubtedly induce considerable dishoarding. To cite one case, it has been estimated that in France alone there are private hoards of not far short of 150 million ounces ($5.25 billion at the present price). Given the present French political structure and the strong position of the franc within the European Economic Community, a doubled gold price could reasonably be expected to tempt out some of the traditional private gold stores.

With this background, let me make some guesses about the amount of gold dishoarding that might take place at a $70 gold price in each of the main categories of private gold absorption.

Traditional hoarding centers. Since the end of World War II, traditional hoarding centers have absorbed some 173 million ounces of gold. If it is assumed that 30 per cent of this amount would be dishoarded (a much smaller proportion than was dishoarded in the 1930s), this would mean a total of about 50 million ounces to be added to official monetary reserves in the five-year period following the price increase.

Jewelry and the arts. One can safely assume that some part of the gold that has gone into "jewelry" in recent years has been held more for the intrinsic value of the gold than the artistic merit of the article. Accordingly, I would guess that at least 10 million ounces (under 7 per cent of the total taken by industry, jewelry, and the arts in the postwar period) would be melted down for the gold content and dishoarded after a price increase.

Other private gold holdings. It seems reasonable to assume that the major part of the gold that in recent years has been absorbed as a protection against currency depreciation would be dishoarded once the currency realignment had taken place, since thereafter there would be a strong incentive to invest in income-earning assets. In the past eleven years, 113 million ounces are estimated to have been diverted into these holdings; if we assume that, say, three-fourths would be dishoarded, this would yield an additional 85 million ounces of gold.

Reduction in future hoarding. Finally, it can reasonably be assumed that such a price increase would sharply reduce the incentive for further hoarding and, accordingly, that at least an additional 15 million ounces a year which are currently being absorbed by hoarding, quasi-jewelry, and other private holdings would flow into official monetary reserves. This would total 75 million ounces in the five-year period.

In summary, the amount of extra gold that might be expected to flow into official reserves during the five years following the introduction of a $70 gold price would be, in millions of ounces:

From traditional hoarding centers   50
From jewelry and the arts   10
From other private holdings   85
  Total estimated release from accumulated private holdings 145
Plus anticipated reduction in future private holdings   75
  Estimated total addition to official gold reserves   220

Although it is not possible to make a reliable estimate of gold dishoarding following a doubled gold price, the foregoing analysis does provide the basis for an informed guess. Under the assumptions made, in the five years after the increase in price, the dishoarding of gold plus the reduction in new hoarding would together yield a total of 220 million ounces of gold. This would be an addition of almost 20 per cent in the physical volume of the Western world's gold reserves and, at $70 an ounce, would increase their value by $15.4 billion.

J. E. Meade, John Exter, Giovanni Magnifico,
Robert A. Mundell, Gardner Patterson, Maurice
Allais, Philip Cortney

CHAPTER X

GOLD AND REFORM: OTHER VIEWS

In addition to those who delivered papers, about two dozen specialists of international distinction participated in the Bologna Center conference and contributed greatly to its effectiveness in exploring various alternatives in international monetary reform. The following statements were selected from an unusually rich exchange of views, either because they raised issues or were concerned with matters, often of a technical nature, which stimulated further thought and discussion. The final statement, by Philip Cortney, occupies a special position. Mr. Cortney, who played a key role in planning the conference, was unable at the last moment to attend because of illness. His statement reflects his reactions after reading the transcript prepared from the tape recording.

R. H.

J. E. Meade*

I speak in danger, I fear, of sounding extremely arrogant, but I shall try my best not to do so. I should say frankly that I feel very sincerely and very strongly that the attention given to liquidity in our discussions is quite out of proportion to the attention that has been given to adjustment. I am saddened at the sight of so many people in such positions of great responsibility, and in such positions of intellectual and academic influence in these matters, spending such a high proportion of time discussing the differences—which I admit are very important, between the various ways of con-

* As professor of political economy at Cambridge University, J. E. Meade is the eminent successor to D. H. Robertson, A. C. Pigou and Alfred Marshall. Before going to Cambridge in 1957, he was for ten years a professor at the London School of Economics. Among his books are *Planning and the Price Mechanism, The Theory of International Economic Policy, A Geometry of International Trade, The Theory of Customs Unions,* and *The Control of Inflation.*

trolling and increasing international liquidity—relative to
the proportion of time which they have given to what in my
view is the much more important problem of how the countries in the free world—the developed, industrialized, liberal countries of the Atlantic community, if you like—
adjust their payments to each other.

I would like to start by giving two examples. Having sat
in an ivory tower for many years, after being for a short
time dressed up as a civil servant, my facts may be all
wrong, but I am pretty sure my theory is right. So I will
give you two illustrations, and if the facts are wrong, just
think of another one. But I have a very strong feeling that
within the last fifteen to twenty years there have been two
outstanding examples of successful domestic macroeconomic
policies in the really powerful countries of the Atlantic
community.

The first is Germany in the period in which there was full
employment, very rapid growth, and really very moderate
price inflation—the textbook case of success, yet coupled
with an enormous surplus in the balance of payments. I
should have been extremely loath to have said to Germany
in such a state of affairs, "You really must inflate; you must
give up this extremely successful policy of combining full
employment, growth, and price stability in order to inflate."

The other very successful policy in recent years, I think,
has been in the United States, where the unemployment
percentage has been very considerably reduced from a level
that many people thought was excessive, and has been reduced by fiscal and monetary policies designed for that purpose, with very, very moderate price inflation. Yet this
country of course has, measured in certain ways, a large
payments deficit. I would not like to say to that country,
"You must deflate." Indeed, I think it would be a great
tragedy. Nor would I say that the United States should give
up the war in Vietnam on balance-of-payments grounds.
Now whether or not one is in favor of the war in Vietnam is a
political problem and should be decided on political grounds.
That you should tell the American troops in Germany that
they must eat only American sandwiches has always seemed
to me to be a form of exchange control that is most perni-
cious, because government expenditures—even more than
private expenditures—should be placed in the cheapest mar-

ket in order to set a good example. Control of capital movements, yes, but not on balance-of-payments grounds. If you believe it wicked that Americans should own French factories, you would think it wicked whether they were in deficit or surplus, surely; if you do not want them to take over foreign industry because you think it is nasty, then say so, but don't recommend such action to correct the balance of payments. I don't believe in these exchange control methods or disguised inconvertibility that we have been witnessing.

I agree with a great deal that Lord Robbins said in his opening address, but I think he overlooked one thing. I am not absolutely convinced myself that fluctuating exchange rates necessarily lead to inflation. Of course one can see the argument: the discipline of feeling that if you inflate you may lose reserves and if you are really bound to a fixed exchange rate, you have got to stop it. But I think there is an argument on the other side which one should not underestimate. It is a fact of life—and we should be looking into the facts of life—that there is a sort of ratchet effect in wage fixing; it is very difficult to get wage rates down, but not difficult to get them up. There is what is known among us professional economists as the Phillips curve; the idea, which I think is basically true, is that the higher the level of demand you have at home, the higher the level of employment you have at home, the more rapidly wage rates are likely to go up. If this be so, and if there comes a point when you get a balance-of-payments disequilibrium with fixed exchange rates, it is infinitely easier to get rid of it by an inflation in the surplus countries than by a deflation in the deficit countries. But this means that the system of fixed exchange rates is *pro tanto* inflationary. One goes around hoping that the surplus countries will inflate (rather than that the deficit countries will deflate) and exerting whatever pressure one can to get them to do so.

There is another matter on which I think I disagree with Lord Robbins, although with great temerity, because quite frankly I am not sure whether I am right or he is right. But I would like to state my view. If exchange rates were more flexible, I do not believe that it would necessarily be true that all contracts in the end would be fixed in terms of one currency. I do not believe that to allow any contracts to be stated in terms of any currency is incompatible with a sys-

tem in which national currencies may vary in relation to each
other. I think it is very doubtful indeed that a British
worker would insist on fixing a wage rate in terms of dollars—looking ahead, at any rate, for the next million years.
In fact, what I am not sure of is whether we are talking of a
million years or forever. I am not quite sure whether, as a
perpetual state, there could be contracts in many currencies,
but I think so. But certainly, so long as there are money
illusions, so long as there are national governments fixing
tax obligations in national currencies, so long as there are
great obstacles and costs of one kind or another, of trading
and of movements of labor, I think that people in one group
will think in terms of one currency and people in another
group in terms of another currency; and it may be much the
easiest way of adjustment to alter the exchange rate.

There are all sorts of proposals which I do not want to go
into now because it would obviously be wrong, for altering
exchange rates in moderate ways, widening "bands," and
introducing what I would like to call a "sliding parity." A
person who calls it a "crawling peg" seems to me to be an
enemy. If I were selling a breakfast food, I would not say,
"Buy the Crawling Wheat"! I think there is a lot in a name;
I do not want to call this idea a crawling peg but rather a
sliding parity—a small but important change.

I still think that it is right and proper, not wrong, to ask:
What is your alternative? Are you going to stop the Vietnam war to put the balance of payments right? Are you
going to control capital movements? Are you going to have
the sandwiches bought in Washington? Are you going to
upset this most successful attempt to stabilize an economy?
I merely ask you what the alternatives are.

But let me now come back to the theme of this conference,
to what I consider to be the very important, but—this is
where I'm so arrogant—still the secondary, problem of exploring the various proposals for revising the *form* of international payments. When I approach this matter, I confess I
do ask myself: What are the forms of reform which would
make alternations in exchange rates easier to carry out? I do
believe this is a major question. For that reason I am in
very strong agreement with Professor Rueff's basic
point—not, I am afraid, on the price of gold, but on what
seems to me the more basic point of both Professor Rueff
and Professor Triffin in wanting to get rid of the gold-

exchange standard, because I think this would make it possible for the United Kingdom and the United States to use the exchange rate properly. I do think that the use of one or two actual national currencies as forms of international payment makes the adjustment mechanism much more difficult, and I do not believe that we would have so much hesitation about using what seems to me the obvious mechanism if it were not for this fact.

So I support Professor Rueff and Professor Triffin in desiring to put an end to the gold-exchange standard. This does not mean that I do not admire and support many of the things that Dr. Bernstein says. I do; and I am sure that his proposal could be developed in the same way, but to me an essential consideration is getting rid of the present burden of these national currencies as a main form of international payment, for the reason I have just indicated.

I am afraid that, having really said that all my betters, if not my elders, have been thinking of the secondary problem when they ought to have been thinking of the primary problem, and having introduced a theme that is not really the subject of this conference, I had better pipe down.

John Exter*

I think it appropriate that I follow Professor Meade, because I have had somewhat the same reaction to the discussion that he has had. We are here, I think, because we are fearful that the present international monetary system will break down. We are discussing possible remedies. The trouble as I see it—and here is where I share Professor Meade's feelings—is that we have discussed these remedies in terms of international reserves or of international liquidity; and this does not seem to me to be the essential problem. The problem has not been the international assets that central banks hold, but the domestic assets. For central banks create money whenever they acquire *any* asset, domestic as well as international.

Thus intellectually I have more sympathy with Professor

---

* As member of a banking mission to Ceylon in the late 1940s, John Exter was so well liked by the Ceylonese that they asked him to become the first governor of the new Central Bank of Ceylon, a post which he held from 1950 until 1953. In 1954 he became vice-president of the Federal Reserve Bank of New York in charge of foreign operations, and since 1960 he has been senior vice-president of the First National City Bank of New York.

Rueff than with the other two panelists. What made the old gold standard work was that central banks did not acquire domestic assets excessively in the nineteenth century. But in the twentieth century, particularly since World War II, they have acquired such assets excessively, and the problem has been that they have acquired them at very unequal rates.

Professor Meade has given us two examples. I should like to say a few words about each. Germany had a remarkable recovery, but it was not based on acquiring domestic assets. In fact, at certain times, the German central bank destroyed money by reducing domestic assets and sterilizing budget surpluses. As it destroyed money, the surplus in the balance of payments was accentuated. The German recovery was built upon a balance-of-payments surplus with virtually no creation of money by the acquisition of domestic assets. I for one like that kind of economics; I thoroughly applaud it.

I am not as loath to criticize my own country as Professor Meade has been, because our recent economic recovery, unlike Germany's, has been based on an acquisition of domestic assets by our Federal Reserve which I should regard as fantastic—almost unbelievable. Since the end of 1957 the Fed has acquired $20 billion of domestic assets, principally in the form of U.S. government securities. (I might say in passing that the Bank of England has continuously acquired domestic assets, too, principally in the form of U.K. government securities.) Not only has the Federal Reserve system been creating money at a very high rate by acquiring U.S. government securities as domestic assets, but, as Professor Rueff has pointed out, foreign central banks have in turn created money by also acquiring U.S. government securities instead of gold as international assets. In other words, our own central bank and foreign central banks have been acquiring U.S. government securities and so creating dollars at the same time. If these practices continue at high rates, the U.S. payments deficit will persist and there is no remedy that can save the system.

The rate of acquisition of domestic assets by our Federal Reserve in the last recovery reached a peak rate of $4.8 billion in one twelve-month period. In addition to that, the Fed created money by also acquiring foreign-currency assets—something that it had not previously done. The foreign currency was acquired through swaps. Thus the creation of money through voluntarily and deliberately acquiring both domestic and foreign-currency assets exceeded $5 billion in one year. During the past year, 1966, this rate slowed down very considerably to $3.2 billion, and monetary expansion was further curtailed by the Fed's decision to raise reserve requirements, which absorbed about $1 billion of commercial bank reserves. I could see the results in my own bank. In 1965 our bank increased its assets by 12 per cent; in 1966, by less than 8 per cent. The slower expansion has been salutary for our balance of payments. Gold losses in 1966 diminished.

Dr. Emminger said this morning that he was terrified by Professor Rueff's proposal to double the price of gold, but the words that have terrified me most in this past week have been the words of my own President in his State of the Union message, in which he pledged that he would use all of the powers of the President to lower interest rates and ease money in the United States. He can fulfill this pledge only if the Federal Reserve acquires more and more domestic assets.

If all central banks were like the National Bank of Switzerland, which has no domestic assets whatsoever, or if they all acted like the Bank of France, which has not added to its domestic assets since 1958, or if they acted as the German central bank has acted during most of the postwar period, I should not be concerned. The problem is that some central banks have not acted in that way. If I were to put a question to our panel, it would be this: How do your schemes deal with this issue? I think I know Professor Rueff's answer. He would try to obtain, by international agreement, a return to the gold standard under rules whereby central banks would observe balance-of-payments discipline and allow a loss of gold to contract the reserve base and not be offset, or more than offset, by acquisitions of domestic assets. But I am not at all sure of the answer that Dr. Triffin or Dr. Bernstein would give to this question.

Giovanni Magnifico*

We have heard from Professor Triffin that if there should be an increase in the price of gold, dollar holdings might

* Giovanni Magnifico is the representative of the Banca d'Italia in London.

become so attractive that it would be difficult to prevent central banks from accumulating them again. The answer to this by Mr. Rueff is that the leading countries should sign an agreement according to which central banks would not do that; they would not accumulate dollars or any other foreign exchange in excess of normal working balances.

I am afraid that such an agreement, even if it could be achieved, might in practice be meaningless, because the foreign exchange accruing to the surplus countries would not need to reach their central banks in order to flow back to deficit countries and thereby inflate their liquidity. That is to say, the foreign exchange might simply remain in the commercial banking system, and commercial banks could invest it in the money markets of the deficit countries so that, even in the system envisaged by Mr. Rueff, we would still have effects similar to those the gold-exchange standard has had, at least up to 1964. This development, moreover, would be merely an extension of recent trends, because in the 1960s various central banks have found ways of encouraging commercial banks to hold more foreign exchange or less foreign exchange, according to circumstances. The agreement to be signed could, of course, forbid commercial banks to engage in these operations, but I think that this would be a very serious infringement upon the freedom of the banking system: it would stultify the efforts and the achievements of this postwar period toward an international money (and capital) market. This is one reason why I cannot support the proposal of Mr. Rueff.

I have a second point, which is on the process of adjustment. With Dr. Emminger and Professor Meade, I am convinced that greater emphasis should be placed on the importance of adjustment. After all, we have had recent cases—for example, the case of Italy in 1963–64 and now, perhaps, of Germany—where the process of adjustment has been carried out with remarkable success. One should remember that the adjustment process is not only an internal responsibility; there is also an international aspect, and here I should like to point out that many of the tensions in the international payments system that have emerged in the past few years would not have been so serious if there had been a larger measure of agreement, among leading industrial countries, on the order of priority among the various objectives of economic policy. I think that if certain countries had insisted less on trying to attain a quasi-absolute price stability and certain other countries had insisted less on forcing rates of growth which the economy could sustain only at the cost of higher price instability, we would have had far less difficulty in the exchange markets than we have experienced.

Robert A. Mundell*

So many issues have been raised during the past two days that I could not possibly deal with all those that interest me. In any case, I realize that the supply of talk exceeds the demand, so that if the price is not to fall, I must be as short as I can.

Mr. Bernstein asked Professor Rueff the difference between a bar of gold and half a bar of gold matched with currencies. There is a difference, a theoretical difference, that was not mentioned by Professor Triffin or Mr. Gilbert or Professor Rueff himself—namely, that gold is nobody's liability and that, when the world price level changes, gold acts as "outside money" while credit money acts as "inside money," as economists on the West Coast of the United States like to say. That is, when you change the price level, the "Haberler-Pigou effect" operates not on the credit component of the money supply but on the gold component. The basic stability of the world economy is therefore based on the "outside money"—the hard-money core that has no counterpart in the liabilities of any other country. I am surprised that Professor Rueff did not mention this point, because I would think it to be a key theoretical element in his argument for an increase in the price of gold. Although I cannot work up any personal enthusiasm for increasing the price of gold, it is best to have all the arguments in its favor carefully laid out.

I would like to turn now to the issue of *adjustment* raised by Professor Rueff and emphasized by Professor Meade. I confess a certain sympathy with his position on this issue. I do not know why it has taken so long for Anglo-Saxon economists to admit the truth of the elementary proposition

---

* A Canadian by birth, Robert A. Mundell is professor of economics at the University of Chicago. He is internationally recognized as one of the leading young economic theorists.

he is making: that there is an adjustment mechanism that is automatically operative under fixed exchange rates if it is allowed to operate. This mechanism has to do with the direct monetary impact of a change in the money supply associated with the deficit or surplus in the balance of payments and with its subsequent impact, even before there has been any change in interest rates, on the level of expenditure. The adjustment process under fixed exchange rates works much better and more smoothly than current theories of the adjustment process imply. In the Anglo-Saxon world the tendency is to assume that Say's "Law" is never relevant, while on the Continent the tendency is to assume that it is always valid. It is neither always valid nor never relevant; sometimes it is and sometimes it is not. I am inclined to believe that it is a useful assumption over the time span in which balance-of-payments problems arise. If that is so, the adjustment mechanism works much better than people on our side of the world are prepared to admit.

I support, therefore, with some qualifications, Mr. Exter's comment about the excessive use of domestic assets to neutralize all the primary and secondary effects of a balance-of-payments deficit. Dr. Emminger also raised that point, and I think that it is very appropriate that Professor Meade, coming from an economy that has had perhaps the most trouble developing or implementing a systematic adjustment mechanism, has also mentioned it. The British have a built-in mechanism of nonadjustment associated with the use of the Exchange Equalization Fund, and they will always run into recurrent balance-of-payments difficulties until they allow at least some part of the monetary effects of a deficit to be felt. The burden of doubt should be given to automaticity unless there are very good reasons, explicitly enunciated, for interfering with it.

I wonder if, in concluding, I might be allowed to put some of the issues in perspective. We should not lose sight of the fact that over the past fifteen years the world economy has been in better shape than in any period over the past fifty years and perhaps over the past few centuries! The gold-exchange standard is much, much better than its reputation. It has its injustices, connected with the serious problem of what Professor Rueff calls "deficits without tears" and what is now often referred to as the "seigniorage problem." The fact that Americans create money that is used as international money and use it to buy up European factories may be an injustice; I grant the theoretical basis of the argument. But in view of the stakes that are involved, this issue is not nearly an important enough consideration to disrupt the structure of the present system, although it is an argument for preserving and improving the system or making a change in it that will make it acceptable to the Europeans in the long run.

Dr. Emminger has argued that the European countries are now fed up with holding additional quantities of dollars but that, by and large, they might be persuaded to hold the amounts of dollars they already have. Professor Triffin has mentioned this point many times before and so has Dr. Bernstein. It is the marginal increments in reserves arising from current surpluses that are now important, and in order to obtain them without an increase in the price of gold or a further extension of the dollar, a reserve substitute is necessary. That is the focus of the argument over liquidity between Dr. Bernstein and Dr. Triffin, and even here I do not find much fundamental disagreement. As Dr. Triffin points out, we emphasize our disagreements, but there is a hard core of agreement. In fact there is no reason, as I see matters, why Rueff's system of adjustment, Triffin's solution of the long-run liquidity problem, and Bernstein's practical steps toward some version of that solution are not acceptable. Dr. Bernstein has an ear bent closely toward acceptable policy solutions, and he himself expressed a concern with the short run. The long run will take care of itself, if we get past the short run with devices that can evolve into acceptable long run solutions. There is a strong probability that Dr. Bernstein's approach would be compatible in the short run with Professor Triffin's in the long run, provided the kinds of Reserve Units we create now are not the kinds that are incompatible with some future organization of deposits in a world central bank. We have to leave the door open for a more imaginative long-run solution, in case there is a lessening of the cold war between parts of Europe and the United States. If that happens, there is some hope for an elegant solution of the type Dr. Triffin has visualized—whether in the form he has planned it or in the spirit in which he has offered it.

In summary, then, I am an enthusiastic supporter of Rueff on the question of adjustment if we are to retain fixed exchange rates, Triffin on the long-run question of liquidity, and Bernstein on the short-run steps needed to take us on the road to Yale in the imminent future.

Gardner Patterson*

Most of what I would have liked to say has already been said. I don't know whether I would have said it, but in many cases I wish I had.

My first point can be made in the form of a question to Professor Rueff, which I hope he may be willing to answer tomorrow. I would like to ask him to tell us a bit about what he thinks the actual effect of his proposal might have been if it had been put into effect ten years ago. I think I know how his plan works in easy cases, but in the tough ones, such as the post-1958 U.S. case, where it is a little hard to fault the policy from most points of view, the effects are more difficult to visualize. One of the major objectives of the Rueff proposal is the forcing of adjustment on deficit countries—or, if you like, the introduction of more monetary discipline. I would really like to know, in a case like the United States, how Professor Rueff thinks his plan might have worked and whether the policies thereby forced on the United States would have been desirable.

One aspect of this conference of special significance is the discussion that has centered on gold. This is a distinctive feature, and anything that can be done to clarify and straighten out the issues relating to gold will be a major contribution. I am glad that there seems to be agreement that many of the things which have been said in this connection are irrelevant. It is good to point this out. I regard as irrelevant the fact that particular gold-producing countries may or may not benefit from a given gold policy. From the standpoint of the international monetary system, the ques-

---

* The career of Gardner Patterson combines rich experience in official and academic life. In the early 1940s he was U.S. Treasury representative in Africa and the Middle East. He has been a professor of economics at Princeton since 1949, and was director of the Woodrow Wilson School of Public and International Affairs from 1957 to 1964. He has served as economic adviser to the American embassies in Israel and in Turkey, as head of a U.S. Economic Survey Mission to Tunisia, and as an adviser to GATT during the Kennedy round.

tion is irrelevant and we ought to dismiss it. I also regard as irrelevant the fortunes or misfortunes of the producing firms themselves. The producers of gold have an annual output of about $1.5 billion. This is fairly small industry in world terms, and it is hardly wise to determine the structure of the future international monetary system on the basis of whether the $1.5 billion goes up, goes down, or stays the same.

Nor am I impressed with the equity argument that for those who hold gold, there is something unfair about the metal being worth no more than it was in 1934 while the price of everything else has gone up. My guess is that the turnover in gold holdings has been so great that the vast bulk now held was not acquired before commodity prices began to rise but was acquired in recent years in exchange for goods and services that were already highly priced.

But there are a large number of relevant questions about gold. A number of these have already been raised, and I think this is a very good thing indeed. I was impressed by the figures that Mr. Busschau gave this morning on what would happen to the output of gold if we were to double the price. Doubling the price of gold is a fairly important step to take, as others here have made abundantly clear. The step is far from trivial. Yet I find, if I have my figures correctly written down, that at the $70 price the annual output of gold by 1980 would be only $2.8 billion. When I consider what might happen between now and 1980 to the level of world trade, which in real terms may well be twice the present level, and when I consider the number of countries that will be involved—because the number that are importantly involved is going to increase in the next fifteen years, and with this increase there will be an additional need for reserves—I wonder whether doubling the price of gold would induce an adequate annual growth in reserves a few years hence. Are we dealing here with something on which we can safely base our international monetary arrangements, even if we accept all the discipline prescribed in Professor Rueff's approach? I would like to hear a bit more discussion about this, for it seems to me a fairly important question. Let me hasten to add that I know Mr. Busschau's figures on future gold production are estimates and that they could go far wrong; nonetheless, I know of no one better qualified than he to make such estimates, and we have to base our policies on the best guesses we can get.

Maurice Allais*

Perhaps I am in a peculiar situation, because I see an element of truth in each of the views which has been expressed, and I believe that a synthesis—I would even venture to say a workable synthesis—is possible. It seems to me that the apparent clashes in the positions of Rueff, Triffin, Bernstein, and Meade are less important than is generally believed.

I would like to recall for you a few very simple facts— facts familiar to everybody, but which appear to me essential. Money is not an end in itself; the ultimate goal is the growth, in real terms, of the economy. If inflation is not a condition for the growth of the economy, we may assert that deflation is absolutely detrimental to growth, and any system of monetary regulation which implies the necessity for certain countries at certain times to take deflationary measures is not a good system. I support Professor Meade in this matter, and I personally believe that flexible exchange rates are a basic condition for a healthy monetary system.

I am afraid that this point, which is the essential one, has not been adequately dealt with in our discussions. We have spoken of the need to fight inflation, but there are no rules of the game on an international level which will make foolish governments wise; and in cases where unwise policies are pursued, the best thing would be for these unfortunate policies to be confirmed as such by exchange rates.

Thus I do not share one view held in common by Rueff, Triffin, and Bernstein: their implicit acceptance of fixed parities as the basis of the monetary system. If we look at what has happened over the last fifty years we see that in one way or another countries have been forced to change the parity of their currencies. This is a fact; one may not like the facts, but they are there. The real choice, therefore, is not between fixed and varying parities—that choice is already made. The actual choice is between big occasional changes, as a re-

* Maurice Allais is a well-known French economic theorist. He is professor of economics at l'École Nationale Supérieure des Mines in Paris and is professor of economic theory at the Institut de Statistique of the University of Paris. He has written widely on theoretical topics.

sponse to big disequilibria, and small continuous changes, which prevent big disequilibria from developing. This is my first point: the important choice is not between gold or paper, but between occasional revisions of exchange rates and continuous revisions.

If we permit exchange rates to adjust continuously, we must choose between freely floating rates and flexible rates, the latter involving certain rules to control erratic fluctuations. I think the second choice is preferable. If it were adopted, there would be some deficits in balances of payments which would have to be financed in one way or another. For that purpose a common money is needed, and Professor Triffin's ideal of moving toward a common money is one which I share completely.

But in the actual state of affairs, that common money can only be gold or paper. On a purely intellectual plane, there is no difference between a paper money whose quantity is limited and gold, as Mr. Bernstein has emphasized. But on the practical or sociological plane, there is an enormous difference. Gold cannot be created out of nothing, but paper money can be printed. Consequently I think the use of gold as an international means of regulating balances of payments is entirely sensible. It is not the ideal solution—in fact, it is open to easy criticism—but I think it is the least impractical of the solutions envisaged at present.

Here I must state my conviction that any mixed gold-paper system combines all the evils of both paper and gold. We must choose not the proper alloy of gold and paper, but either gold *or* paper. That is the only rational choice.

Now if, for sociological, political, and practical reasons, we consider gold the only suitable vehicle for settling international balances, then the question arises: What price for gold? I was very much swayed by Dr. Emminger's presentation, one of the most intelligent cases that I have heard against any revaluation of gold. But there is one question to which he made no reference and which he did not answer in any way; and that is the question of the progressive accumulation of gold over the last twenty years by certain central banks. We may lament this fact; we may say that it is irrational to pile up gold, but the fact remains that the gold reserves of the Group of Ten, excluding the United States and Great Britain, have grown in recent years at an annual rate of about 9 per cent whereas world gold production has grown at an annual rate of only about 1.3 per cent. This situation cannot continue, and, whatever the value of Dr. Emminger's arguments, we must deal with the problem.

I think the only conclusion to be drawn from a disinterested examination of the facts of the past is that sooner or later, under orderly or disorderly conditions, it will be necessary to raise the price of gold. The question, therefore, is not one of retaining the present price or raising it, but of raising it in an orderly way or in a state of disorder.

If we raise the price of gold, how much should we raise it? I think doubling the price is not the right answer. Those who argue that it is appear to assume that the increase made—or ratified, shall we say?—in 1934 was correct. In the years immediately after 1934, however, there was an excess of gold liquidity which was widely criticized at the time. I think the only satisfactory basis for comparison is 1913. Taking that year as a base, we are led to conclude that to maintain the parity of gold relative to other goods, we should raise the price, not by 100 per cent but by 50 per cent. And politically speaking, it would of course be much easier to raise the price by 50 per cent than by 100 per cent.

Some of the strongest arguments presented here against raising the price of gold have really been arguments not against raising the price, but against *doubling* it. It has been concluded that such a big increase would place us in a highly inflationary situation. I think that is correct. If we were to double the price of gold, taking into account a probable dishoarding of $6 billion, there would undoubtedly be considerably inflationary pressure. With an increase of 50 per cent, on the other hand, the objections concerning inflation lose much of their force.

If the price is raised by 50 per cent, should it be stabilized there? I would say no. I think we should avoid repeating the error made after World War I, when in 1925 the pound sterling re-established the prewar price of gold, and we should avoid the error made after World War II, when no change was made in the dollar price of gold established in 1934. We ought to plan for a continual and regular increase in the price of gold. I think an annual increase of 1 per cent would be sufficient. This would prevent any deflation whatever and at the same time would provide no motive for hoarding.

There is one last point about gold I would emphasize. I am partial to gold, but I think we must recognize that gold is not an ideal standard. Mr. Bernstein has circulated a table of price movements in the nineteenth century and, reading nineteenth century history, one encounters numerous complaints about price movements engendered by fluctuations in the world supply of gold. I personally believe that the only really satisfactory standard from the standpoint of assuring a stable price level would be a composite commodity standard.

But must we conclude from this that gold has no value? That would be a serious error. Gold has value, first of all, as a means of settling international balances and, secondly, as a form of insurance which citizens can take out against foolish policies of their governments. I am among those who think it desirable to permit an open market in gold similar to those of France and Switzerland.

In summary, I think that there are two objectives toward which we might desire to move. The first is to lend more flexibility to the international monetary system. This implies enlarging the permissible margin of variation in exchange rates. We are prevented from taking such action only by the Articles of the International Monetary Fund, which need only a very slight modification to render the system much more adaptable. The second objective, which I share with Professor Triffin, is the creation of an international currency. An international currency would have numerous advantages—especially the disappearance of key currencies; if all national currencies were linked to the same international currency, then changes in exchange rates would become much easier and cause far less disturbance.

The question is what that currency might be. At present, the only possibility is gold. Perhaps in a few decades, when men become more rational, we might envisage an international paper currency. It is an ideal we must on no account abandon. We have succeeded well in demonetizing gold on the domestic level, so why not on the international level? For the present, however, a global paper money can only be a beautiful dream.

This, then, is my synthesis, in which I find much common ground with other positions presented around this table.

*Philip Cortney**

In my remarks on gold and international monetary reform, I would like to concentrate on what I regard as a dangerous monetary error—an error which helps to explain why the Great Depression of 1929–33 was so deep and so prolonged, and an error which we appear determined to repeat once more.

I share the view of Rist, Jacobsson, Schumpeter, and Hicks that the crisis of 1929 was a normal cyclical crisis which would not have been particularly serious had it not coincided with a deep drop in prices. But why the deep drop in prices after 1929? In 1929 the world price level in terms of gold was about 50 per cent higher than in 1914. This price level was a sequel to the war—the result of paper money inflation to finance the war and of the shortage of manufactured goods both during and for some years after the war. The means of payment had been increased to four or five times (and in some countries much more than five times) their prewar volume; and the war and its aftermath had also resulted in a huge accumulation of debts, both national and international.

The great monetary error after World War I was to stabilize the gold content of the dollar and of the pound at their prewar parities, while at the same time making every effort—by adopting the gold-exchange standard and by abnormally expanding credit in the United States—to stabilize commodity prices at a level much higher than before the war. Meanwhile, the world gold production per year, instead of being at the higher level required by the higher commodity prices, fell from $250 million in 1914 to $230 million in 1929.

The monetary error of the 1920s had two serious consequences. First, the gold base of the international monetary system became inadequate to meet all the domestic and international requirements put on it and, beginning some time in 1930–31, the monetary and price instability became more and more disturbing. It is significant that between 1924 and

* For many years president of Coty Incorporated and Coty International, Philip Cortney has long been keenly interested in international monetary problems, on which he has written extensively. He is vice-president of the Monetary Commission of the International Chamber of Commerce.

1934 the United States was unable to increase its stock of gold. The situation had all the appearances of a "scarcity of gold" (and was so characterized by many) while, in fact, it was the consequence of the monetary error I have just described.

J. R. Hicks, in his book *A Contribution to the Theory of the Trade Cycle,* gives the following explanation of the severity of the Great Depression:

Really catastrophic depression . . . is likely to occur when there is profound monetary instability—when the rot in the monetary system goes very deep . . . . My interpretation of the Great Depression [is that] the slump impinged upon a monetary situation which was quite exceptionally unstable . . . . The monetary system of the world had never adjusted itself at all fully to the change in the level of money incomes which took place during and after the war of 1914–18; it was trying to manage with a gold supply, which was in terms of wage units extremely inadequate.

But a similar situation prevails today. Bernstein has recently expressed the opinion that "we probably already have a shortage of aggregate reserves, particularly with the serious depletion of the net reserves of the United States and the United Kingdom."

The second serious consequence of the monetary error of the 1920s was that gold production was at too low a level to bring about the necessary expansion of gold reserves and of money supply required in a dynamic world. The reason, of course, was that the cost of producing gold had increased substantially while the price of gold in terms of the dollar and sterling remained at the 1914 figure.

In a famous paper presented in 1946 at the twenty-fifth anniversary of the National Bureau of Economic Research, Per Jacobsson showed that the relation between the yearly amount of gold available for monetary purposes and the yearly increase in national income was 1 to 11 in 1913, while it was 1 to 30 in 1929. From these figures Jacobsson drew the conclusion that current gold production contributed less to sustaining prices in 1929 than in 1913. This unfavorable development surely played a key role in accounting for the disastrous fall in prices, which was closely associated with the monetary convulsions from 1931 onward and with the paralysis of so much of the international credit system.

The conclusion that Per Jacobsson drew from the events

of the 1920s was formulated at the end of his address: "We must watch carefully the signs of the times to ensure that we do not again commit the mistake of trying to stabilize in gold [prices and the gold content of currencies] at an unsuitable level."

The lessons we can learn from the economic and monetary events of the period from 1870 (when practically all of Europe adopted the gold standard) to 1933 seem clear:

1. In normal times (by which I mean a period not influenced by a great war), where there is a link, even nonrigid, between global gold reserves and the global monetary circulation, with gold fixed at an appropriate price, there arises a state of dynamic but stable equilibrium between the monetary circulation, the level of commodity prices, and the production of gold, while the production of goods increases with rare interruptions.

2. If the equilibrium is disturbed by a great war it is essential, in re-establishing the link—however loose or elastic—between gold reserves and the monetary circulation, to set the price of gold at the right value in order to obtain an adequate global monetary gold stock and an adequate annual increase in world gold reserves.

3. After the money and price inflation accompanying a great war, any monetary system based on gold—including our present IMF system—is in great danger of collapsing unless the new price of gold has been correctly established.

The $35 price of gold was chosen by the United States after the upheaval of World War I and the Great Depression in the light of the circumstances—prices, debts, costs, and so on—prevailing at that time. It is completely unrealistic in 1967, even though it has been possible, thus far, to keep the present monetary system from collapsing. For the time being, the system is kept in operation by the inflationary monetary policy of the United States and its chronic, abnormal balance-of-payments deficits, which have supplied the rest of the world with dollar reserves and dollar liquidity (while at the same time undermining confidence in the dollar). The present unstable, precarious, and dangerous situation is being artificially maintained by the common fear of all governments of "upsetting the applecart."

The United States has stated repeatedly that it is opposed

to a rise in the price of gold—as if, in the final analysis, the price of gold depended on its independent decision or will. Studies of this question lead me to the conclusion, however, that it is no longer in the power of the United States to prevent a rise in the gold price if we wish to forestall a crisis similar to that of 1931–33 or the drift into a completely controlled economy.

Lord Robbins, Jacques Rueff, Edward M. Bernstein,
Robert Triffin

CHAPTER XI

CONCLUDING OBSERVATIONS

In his role as moderator, Lord Robbins opened the final session with a statement of the issues as they appeared in the light of the discussion up to that point, of the main areas of agreement and disagreement, and of the unresolved questions he wished to have considered by Messrs. Bernstein, Rueff, and Triffin in their concluding remarks. The statement by Lord Robbins appears below, followed by the concluding statements of the three plan authors in the order in which they were made.

R. H.

Lord Robbins

Let me hasten to remove any impression that I am now going to pass judgment in a comprehensive way on our deliberations. If a summary is intended to provide a guide for action, I am really the last person who is competent to do it at this stage, and the last person who would be willing to do it. I have not served a very long period of my life as a public servant, but I have served long enough to know that you don't make up your mind on concrete policies without being seized of a great deal more detail and background than it would be possible for me to command in this context. Therefore, all that I want to do to start the debate is to make a survey of some of the highlights of what has been said, and to try to indicate broad areas of agreement and disagreement.

To begin with, I think that we should recollect that, in the course of our discussions, we have had very valuable surveys of the factual situation. First, I should like to pay tribute to Milton Gilbert's extremely able marshaling of the complicated body of facts in regard to the growth of reserves. And I should equally like to pay tribute to Dr. Busschau for his fascinating exposition of the possibilities with

143

respect to gold production in the future. Dr. Busschau is one of the greatest experts in the world on this subject; and it was a great privilege to get his slant on those possibilities.

As regards the facts of the past which are significant, there seem to me to be two salient conclusions. First, it emerged from Milton Gilbert's survey how much has already been done in one way or another to provide for an increase of reserves since the beginning of the 1960s. Any suggestion that the world has been unduly hampered to date by the limitations of existing arrangements, including the Bretton Woods Agreement, is belied by the facts. I always suspected that, when the crunch came, Dr. Bernstein would be able to find ingenious interpretations of rules which would provide far more elbowroom than the world was given to suppose when the final acts were promulgated—and that, in fact, has happened.

At the same time—that is the second conclusion in this context—I suppose one must concede that the fact that all this has been done over and above the normal routine does indicate the existence of a problem; and Milton Gilbert gave as his opinion that the existence of the sort of problem we have to discuss at this conference had begun to make itself palpable as regards practical action by the beginning of this decade.

As for the future, again I see two outstanding items of information which have revealed themselves. First, the probable decline in gold production at the present price of gold; and second, the fascinating vista of the degree of increase in production, after an interval of perhaps three to five years, if the price were doubled. In this connection, I can't resist from alluding to Gardner Patterson's important query regarding the latter point. He suggested that if the gold supply were to increase on the scale which Dr. Busschau's calculations seem to make probable, it would take care of the requirements of expanding international trade for only a comparatively short time. He wondered, therefore, if what was proposed in that connection—the once-for-all change—would really do the job. I won't pronounce on that, but it is certainly a matter to which we might give more attention.

With regard to the results up to this point of our discussion about the broad conception of the future problem, I see important areas of agreement and some areas of disagreement. I think we all agree that the facts point to some future shortage of reserves. I haven't observed any sign of complacency in that respect—no suggestion that we can just roll along without doing anything. I think we also agree about the very great dangers that seem to be implicit in the present position, in particular the danger that apprehensions of the future and independent actions by certain authorities may touch off chain reactions that might rapidly lead to a position of disorderly crisis.

I think we agreed further that the gold-exchange standard has reached what may be called the quantitative limit of its usefulness. This is not to say we are all agreed that we want to abolish the gold-exchange standard, but I think we all agree that an extension—at any rate, in the circumstances likely in the next few years—is not an event we should regard as being either likely or useful.

We have not agreed about the utility of this particular mechanism in the past. Monsieur Rueff and Mr. Triffin in different ways have stressed its evil effects on the adjustment problem. Others, I suspect, think that it hasn't worked too badly to date and that although in recent years it has begun to creak, yet in view of general growth of production and trade since the war, the availability of dollars on a large scale has not necessarily had bad effects. Most, I think, agree that we must not look in that direction for further help now.

As regards the future of the gold-exchange standard, some of us wish to see it entirely liquidated. Monsieur Rueff would like to see it liquidated because he can't believe that adjustment will be safeguarded while it exists: he can't believe that, while the gold-exchange standard exists, the central banks can, or will, so conduct their affairs as to produce a tendency to international equilibrium. My great friend James Meade would like to liquidate it because the existence of the gold-exchange standard presents certain obstacles to and complications in the carrying out of certain reforms in exchange rate policy which he regards as desirable. Some, however—and I underline the notable contribution of Dr. Emminger in this respect—think that if confidence in the dollar and the pound is restored, the gold-exchange standard might continue to exist in a restricted form, perhaps, and even discharge useful functions.

This leads me to the next item of broad agreement—
namely, that the U.S. and U.K. deficits must be cured if
there is to be any hope of reform in any direction. There is
not complete agreement how far this should go—I don't
know how many members of the conference would wish to
see the United States once more running a surplus. Nor
have we discussed at any length how this readjustment is to
take place. James Meade implied that, at fixed exchange
rates, the readjustment could only be expected by a damaging contraction of expenditure in the United States. Some of
us, I suspect, are less pessimistic than that—I suspect that
James Meade imagines that the deficits will not be cured
unless there is a change in the exchange rate. Most of us, I
imagine, share Mr. Exter's dismay—or, if "dismay" is too
strong a word, apprehension—at the American President's
announcement that he intends to use his power to produce
some downward movement in interest rates, a policy that
certainly would not be conducive to the improvement of the
U.S. balance.

From all this, surely, there does emerge a considerable
agreement about the two essentials of a final solution. A
final solution must provide for effective adjustment of disequilibria in balances of payments, and it must provide more
liquidity than is in prospect with present arrangements. I
imagine that James Meade would agree with that, although
I expect that he would urge that, if there were more flexibility in exchange rates, then to that extent the necessity for
massive mobilization of liquidity, in the way we have been
discussing it, would diminish.

Then finally—still on the plane of broad generalization—I
think I detect a considerable degree of agreement that the
machinery of the Fund alone is not likely to provide a
solution. Professor Dowd, indeed, made a passionate plea
that the voice of the underdeveloped world be heard in
deliberations on these difficult problems, and no doubt many
of us sympathize with the underlying sentiment. Nevertheless, having sat through meetings with representatives of
the underdeveloped countries when problems of this sort
were being discussed, I myself should find it difficult in such
contexts to be very optimistic about the degree of help that
would be yielded to technical solutions of these problems.
And though, on the whole, I have not heard frontal attacks

on the IMF as at present constituted, I do sense a certain consensus of opinion that the present problems require for their initiative and execution tighter, smaller bodies. In spite of protests that have from time to time been made in the world at large, I imagine that there are a good many of us who are quite thankful that the Group of Ten exists.

Now let me turn to greater detail as regards plans and the differences between plans. We have been discussing three plans: Monsieur Rueff's plan, Mr. Triffin's plan, and Mr. Bernstein's plan. I confess I rather share James Meade's disappointment that more time has not been available for discussing the plans that proceed on the basis of increasing in one way or another the flexibility of exchange rates. Not that I find myself in very great agreement with him on this, but, as I said, I do think that one ought not to underestimate the weight of high-powered technical opinion which does favor solutions of that sort in greater or lesser degree.

But let me confine my observations to the three plans that were discussed. In my capacity as conciliator, I shall begin by underlining the very considerable agreement, as regards both formal objectives and diagnosis, which underlies all three. I must say that I have been struck by Monsieur Rueff's continual emphasis on the adjustment problem; and I suspect that if he could be convinced that the other plans would work practically to its solution, his feelings about the price of gold would not prevent him from agreeing with them. Similarly, we have all witnessed the agreement of Messrs. Triffin and Bernstein on the necessity for adjustment and for continuous adjustment.

Nevertheless, of course, on this plane there emerge considerable differences of opinion. First, there is the outstanding difference of opinion between Monsieur Rueff on the one side, and Messrs. Bernstein and Triffin on the other, on the role of gold and the possibility for substitutes for gold in international reserves. These differences are, in the nature of things, sharp where practical action is concerned. In the end, you have to choose one of these plans and reject the others. Second, differences have emerged between Messrs. Bernstein and Triffin on the nature and the distribution of the proposed substitutes for gold. These seem to me to be the outstanding differences, and perhaps I could refine them a little by focusing on the present stage of the discussion, with

particular reference to what Monsieur Rueff has said. I
think I can bring out best what has happened, and what has
not happened, by a little recapitulation here.

If I interpret him correctly, Monsieur Rueff's emphasis is
on the prime necessity for adjustment on the one hand and
on the bad effects of the gold-exchange standard as a mechanism of adjustment on the other. To see his proposals in
proper perspective, one must regard what he has to say
about the price of gold as subservient to the pursuit of
adjustment and the diagnosis of the bad effects of the
gold-exchange standard. Since most of us are agreed on the
necessity for adjustment and on the possible bad effects of
the gold-exchange standard, objections to Monsieur Rueff's
position must be to the expedients or remedies that he proposes and not to his aims. These objections, as I have lis-
tened to them, seem to fall into different categories.

The first set of objections relates to the actual practical
difficulties of putting his proposals into motion. Whether
one agrees with him or disagrees with him, I think one must
concede that Dr. Emminger's observations in this respect
have great force and cogency. I personally am immensely
impressed by his exposition of the practical difficulties of
negotiating a change of this sort. One is led to ask—and I
hope that Monsieur Rueff will be able to expatiate a little on
this—whether one must conclude that such a change can
come about only because of a crisis. Up to this point, the
balance of argument seems to indicate that as a very real
danger.

A second set of objections is based on the dangers of
inflation. We have already had a very illuminating exposition on that issue from Monsieur Rueff himself. I say "illuminating" because it did open my eyes to certain aspects of
Monsieur Rueff's conception of the functioning of the gold
standard which I was vaguely aware of before but which I
had never heard formulated quite so explicitly. Monsieur
Rueff's position is that although he would concede that there
are dangers of inflation, he feels that the instruments available to the central banks—quite apart from the special
measures that he proposes for the repayment of claims and
loans—should enable them to avoid those dangers. And on
this I noted that Mr. Bernstein, always willing to make
intellectual concessions where he feels intellectual conces-

sions are due, did say that one ought not completely to rule out the possibility of agreements that would accomplish this aim. Nevertheless, I do still feel that both the general implications of this change and what has been said in greater detail leave me with the uncomfortable feeling that the order of magnitude of the proposed change in the price of gold does carry with it serious dangers of inflation. Perhaps even at this late hour Monsieur Rueff can say more to reassure us.

The third group of objections depends upon what I call the once-for-allness of the proposal. It is commonly felt, I think, that—in contrast to this quality—the fundamental desideratum is a reserve-creating mechanism permitting gradual change and gradual adaptation to the needs of the world situation as it unfolds. I think it is generally agreed that discontinuous changes in the price of gold would be undesirable. Professor Allais, however, suggested continuous small changes. I have not detected any support for this proposal, but it certainly has to be included in the list of possibilities.

Finally, of course, and underlining the position of many of us, there is a failure to be convinced that there may not be some superior authority in alternative plans—plans that avoid the dangers of catastrophic disturbance of the kind Dr. Emminger has pointed out and plans that permit a future development of an integrated world system. Monsieur Rueff's contention, I take it, is that he sympathizes with such plans but finds them practically unacceptable.

What about the other plans? Here we are evidently on extremely technical ground, where I should not be able to hold my own in arguments with either Mr. Bernstein or Mr. Triffin. But shall I give great offense, shall I alienate friendship, if I say that I think they have much in common, very much in common, via-à-vis Monsieur Rueff? Therefore I have been inclined to talk about them together. In my notes they are "B & T." But there are divergencies, and they are divergencies which I hope we shall have an opportunity to hear discussed a little further this morning.

First, I think—and I am not sure about this—that there is some divergence in ultimate tendencies. I have the suspicion that Mr. Triffin's plan is more ambitious than Mr. Bernstein's, although Mr. Triffin has assured me that he does not want to be regarded as very ambitious at this stage, and I know from long acquaintance that Mr. Bernstein is at heart a utopian idealist. So I think this is a small difference, although it does appear from time to time when they are discussing particular questions. But both admit that we cannot go all the way at once, and I trust that I will offend neither in suggesting that there can be a convergence of view on what needs to be done in the next two or three years.

There is, however, a further difference, which perhaps in the broad perspective that I have been discussing in these remarks is not so important, but which has considerable relevance to any technical discussion—namely, a divergence on the technique of allocation of the new reserves that they propose to create. Mr. Bernstein relies upon criteria based perhaps—he is very tentative on this—on the quota structure of the Fund. He hopes to get adjustment by wise advice and pressure from the appropriate authorities, whereas Mr. Triffin seeks to bring the adjustment mechanism more within the confines of his scheme for a world central bank. While I don't want to take words out of his mouth, I imagine Mr. Bernstein's reply to the criticism that his criteria for reserve allocation are a bit arbitrary would be that, after all, one has to have some criteria and is more likely to get away with this one—and that, in the end, although it is logically imperfect compared with Mr. Triffin's proposal, the degree of imperfection is not very important and practically it may be easier to push this thing through. But I am now venturing in the field of conjecture, and I ought to stop because, after all, we have the performers here and they should carry on.

I wind up, therefore, by suggesting that, as I see things, there are at least three fundamental desiderata to be mentioned some time in our concluding discussion. I think that we should have explicit replies—if I may use my shorthand notes—by B & T to Monsieur Rueff's charge of lack of realism. I think I personally should like to hear a further development by B & T individually—not collectively—of their conceptions of the very next steps; and, finally, I should like to hear further comments by Monsieur Rueff on Dr. Emminger's critique of the immediate dangers in negotiating his proposals and, in this connection, some reply by Monsieur Rueff to Dr. Patterson's extremely fascinating inquiry: What would have happened if the plan had come into operation ten years ago?

Jacques Rueff

I am most grateful to Lord Robbins for having put the finger on what is for me the main question: the process of adjustment. And I feel greatly encouraged, because many friends around this table seem to share that view. This has not been true in the past. As I think Professor Meade said, much attention has been given to the need for liquidity and very little attention to the need for adjustment. In this connection, I would like to reply to the accusation of lack of realism. I would emphasize a very simple point: without foreign exchange, one cannot spend foreign exchange; when a treasury is deprived of foreign exchange and has been informed that it will not receive foreign credit, there is nothing to do but to close the door. I hope you recognize that this really is realism! Anything else is a pure dream; the plans may be excellent, but without foreign exchange they are finished. So the problem is to create a situation in which you have a permanent equilibrium in the balance of payments.

Here I must thank Mr. Patterson for his intriguing question, because it will induce me to develop what seems to me the essence of this matter. He asked, "What if your proposal had been applied ten years ago?" I will answer in a most provocative way: There would have been no deficit in the U.S. balance of payments. In the past, when there was an effective system of payments, adjustment always took place promptly, mainly through changes in the balance of trade. The rich countries—the countries with a large income from foreign investments, shipping, and other sources—typically had a balance of trade in heavy deficit. The poor countries, having borrowed abroad, normally had a trade surplus. For example, in 1930, France, Great Britain, Holland, Belgium, and Switzerland all had a big deficit in their trade balances. On the other hand, Germany, which was in poor condition, as well as Poland, Rumania, Hungary, and Bulgaria—which were poor countries with great internal needs—all had a big surplus in the balance of trade.

I could cite many other examples, but time does not permit.[1] Let me give you only one more, which is most strik-

[1] These and other cases are discussed in greater detail in Mr. Rueff's book *The Balance of Payments* (New York: Macmillan, 1967).

ing—the case of France before World War I. France, being
an old and rich country with large investments abroad, had
for many years had a deficit in its balance of trade. Between
1870 and 1914, the French trade balance was in deficit every
year except four. Which were the four years? You may
remember that in 1870 we lost a war with Germany, and,
according to the Treaty of Frankfurt of 1871, we had to pay
Germany 5 billion gold francs, which were transferred in
the years 1872, 1873, 1874, and 1875. The four—the only
four—years in which the French trade balance was in surplus were exactly these same years, 1872 through 1875. I
verified the same result with respect to German reparations
after World War I in a long discussion I had with Lord
Keynes, which was published in the *Economic Journal* in
1929.

But let us return to the U.S. case, for it is most illuminating. The United States, with great generosity, has made
enormous payments abroad—Marshall funds, other aid, military expenditures, and also large investments—all requir-
ing great transfers and implying a large surplus in its
balance of trade. There has, in fact, been a very large export
surplus, but it has not been quite large enough to achieve
equilibrium in the balance of payments. What has been
missing? Actually, only a small fraction of the required
amount was not effectively transferred, and this was not
transferred because, under the gold-exchange standard, it
was returned to the United States. This small fraction,
really a minor amount in relation to the amount actually
transferred, corresponds to the increase in dollar balances
and the various new devices that Milton Gilbert has told us
about—swaps, Roosa bonds, and so on.

My conclusions are not revolutionary at all. They are
what professors have taught for many years. They are valid
not only in theory but also in practice, and the sensitivity of
the adjustment mechanism is so great that, where it is
permitted to operate, I have never seen a delay of more than
three months between cause and effect.

Thus I would reply to Mr. Patterson that I am quite sure
that if my proposal had been applied ten years ago—that is,
if there had been no gold-exchange standard, but real payments for the whole amount of the deficit in the balance of
payments—the export surplus of the United States would

have been just a little greater, which would have suppressed the deficit and would also have suppressed the reason for meetings of this kind, because our present problems would not have arisen.

This does not mean that the United States is to blame for the present situation. The Americans are not the authors of the gold-exchange standard. They have never asked for it; they are its victims. The gold-exchange standard was never planned; it is not the result of a scientific study aimed at improving the international monetary system. It is simply the result of certain central banks preferring to have an income-yielding asset instead of gold. Some central banks have not even realized that they were on a gold-exchange standard. When I published my article in 1961, "The Danger for the West: The Gold-Exchange Standard," two of my central banking friends asked me, "Do you really believe that we are *not* on the gold standard?" Their question could only mean that they had not realized what a revolution had occurred in the operation of the world payments mechanism.

Some may ask, "Why a reform? Everything is all right now; why not continue?" Well, let me answer that when somebody falls from the tenth floor of a building, everything is all right until he reaches the ground! In the present situation, which is deteriorating month by month, we are heading for the ground, and that is the reason for reform, even though arrangements, for the time being, may appear to be satisfactory. I would add that in every case of a banking catastrophe, everything seems all right until the last moment.

My two friends, Mr. Bernstein and Mr. Triffin, agree with me on the need for reform, and I would now like to say a few words about their ingenious proposals. From what I have read of their very elaborate plans, I understand that in both cases it is a kind of inconvertible currency they have in mind—a currency either totally or partially inconvertible into gold. I am convinced that, whatever the wisdom of the authorities, the creation of an *ad hoc* inconvertible currency makes international balance very unlikely. In 1930 I was financial attaché in London, and I studied the policy of the Bank of England before the crisis. I have also looked at the recent policy of the Federal Reserve Board. In both cases, the monetary effect of an outflow of gold was canceled by the creation of credit. It was not by deliberate will that this happened; it was the natural result of pressures resulting from the market. Of course the central bank could have opposed these pressures by a deliberate discount policy, but that was politically and technically difficult, if not humanly impossible. As long as monetary creations are independent of gold movements, which seems to me the case in the Triffin and Bernstein proposals to the extent that these involve the creation of an inconvertible currency, there is little hope that there will be international balance.

My next point concerns the allocation of new reserves. New reserves, of course, are a free gift. If Mr. Bernstein gives the new reserves to everybody, as he proposes, the countries in surplus will have an increase in their liquidity, and that will either have no effect or will raise the problem of which he has warned us—of inflation resulting from unwanted liquidity. Such an allocation seems to me purely arbitrary, and I do not think there is a rational solution along these lines.

I have the same feeling about the rate of reserve creation. Here there seems to me to be no criterion whatever. Mr. Triffin in his plan wants reserves to grow from 3 to 5 per cent a year, and Mr. Bernstein suggests an annual growth of 3 per cent. But how do we know whether this is too little or too much? It could only be the right rate by pure chance. The production of gold, on the other hand, is regulated by the movement of commodity prices. If the price of gold were established at a realistic level, there is every reason to believe that gold production would be influenced in such a way as to provide the appropriate growth in reserves.

But the price of gold must be at the right level. If the monetary system is functioning in a continuous way, it maintains all elements of the economic situation—particularly prices—at a level which corresponds to the amount of liquidity in the world. The question of a *change* in the price of gold emerges only if there has been a long period, such as we have had after the two world wars, during which gold has not been permitted to function properly. In World War I, the U.S. price level increased by 50 per cent. In such cases one has only one choice—either to **reduce** the price level to a level corresponding to the old price of gold or to raise the price of gold to a level corresponding to the new price level. Of course, it is purely academic to imagine that the price level could be reduced by 50 per cent in the United States, and that is why I think there is no acceptable solution except a rise in the price of gold.

The plans of Mr. Bernstein and Mr. Triffin are extremely subtle, intelligent, of course, and complicated. From my experience as a public servant, I am convinced that the instruments which one administers have to be simple, even rough, and easy to understand. I don't believe that one can move the earth with the delicate instruments of a surgeon. And I don't think that with such instruments one can go very deeply into the realities of human behavior. One must have very simple instruments, and the proposal which I present to you is of this kind. It is rough; it is efficient; and it is simple. On the contrary, the plans of my two friends are subtle and highly ingenious, but complicated. That seems to me a strong argument for preferring my approach.

Now I come to the point raised by Dr. Emminger: the difficulty of negotiations. Let me tell you, this problem is not so difficult. In 1958 we had a negotiation with European central banks about the re-establishment of convertibility. It was conducted in great secrecy without any trouble. In 1938 I personally negotiated the Tripartite Agreement with the United States and the United Kingdom. It was possible to conduct these negotiations very secretly. On one occasion, Mr. Morgenthau, who was then the U.S. Secretary of the Treasury, was returning to the United States; I accompanied him from Le Havre to Southampton by ship—I think it was the *Normandie*—and we had a conversation which nobody knew of. In 1935, when we were negotiating an agreement with Germany on the Saar, I always met with the head of the German delegation in a Dutch museum. You know, there are armchairs facing the pictures, and there we discussed secret matters regularly for three months. No journalist in the world ever knew that those discussions were taking place.

So I am confident that if we were conscious of the need of agreement, it could be obtained secretly and efficiently. But the problem is to make the need conscious and, in particular, to make it conscious in the United States. As long as matters remain as they are, nothing will be possible before the pressure of events has forced action. I agree with Dr. Emminger that the prospects for an agreement before a crisis are very weak. When issues are difficult, they are rarely settled by men but rather by events. In the meantime, there will be more foreign exchange control, more regulations, perhaps import quotas—measures that really are very bad for the welfare of the world, particularly when undertaken by a country of such importance as the United States.

What is likely, if a reform on the lines I have suggested is not applied before a crisis, is that we shall continue to drift along until it is apparent that the demand for gold can no longer be met. At that time, there will be an embargo on gold and, under the umbrella of this embargo, it will be possible to settle the matter.

I hope that then, at least, the question will be settled quickly—I mean, in a few days. We have had many experiences of this kind, particularly in connection with devaluation. The scenario is always the same. After the close of the stock exchange on Friday evening, the government decrees an embargo on gold or foreign exchange and, after that, the show can begin. What I would like is for agreement to be reached so quickly that on Monday morning it will be possible to re-open the stock exchange and to re-establish freedom of payments at the new price of gold.

The measures I have proposed are easy to understand; central bankers are accustomed to much more complicated negotiations. They meet regularly and know each other well. Agreements among central banks are so common that it is a little absurd to exaggerate the difficulty. I should add, finally, that nothing would have to be negotiated with respect to the regulations of the International Monetary Fund, because the Fund Articles, by authorizing a uniform change in par values, have made wise provision for exactly the reform that I feel is so badly needed.

I still hope that such a reform, for which I have energetically strived for six years, will be adopted before a crisis. If not, we shall have a painful and dangerous experience which a little more statesmanship could have easily avoided. In the meantime, let us prepare, at least, to make that crisis as brief and as painless as possible.

Edward M. Bernstein

I would like to start by saying how much I have enjoyed this discussion. Generally speaking, I find meetings on international monetary reform very trying, because I have to repeat what I have said in many other places and because I hear the same questions and the same arguments. What has made this an unusually good discussion is the bluntness with which we have approached the gold question and, I think, the reasonable attitude that the participants—and especially the advocates of a change in the price of gold—have shown. Of course, we could not have achieved such success if we had not had such a fine moderator and leader as Lord Robbins and such an excellent chairman as Willard Thorp.

It is too bad that we can't discuss every important aspect of a question at the same conference. Clearly, the adjustment process is very important. In a sense, indeed, adjustment is the most important question, because the only reason for having a discussion on reserves is to make adjustment easier.

I believe with Mundell that, by and large, the adjustment process in the postwar world has worked reasonably well. By that I mean that balance-of-payments disequilibria have been remedied without prolonged depressions and big deflations. The United States and the United Kingdom are perhaps exceptions. But even in the case of the United States, it is important to note that there the adjustment process did work in a very important direction: We increased our export surplus of goods and services very sharply from 1959 to 1964. The difficulty is that in the same period we increased our private capital outflow on a fantastic scale, while of course the government also increased its spending for aid and military purposes. Unfortunately, it is not as easy to get a natural and simple adjustment in the investment accounts—and certainly not in the aid and military accounts—as in trade.

I do agree that if settlement had been exclusively in gold, the United States would have restored its balance of payments sooner. I am not sure that this would have been better for the rest of the world. A deflation in the United States would not have been good for the rest of the world, nor would a cut in aid. It might have been better for the United

States, however, to have taken the extra measures that adjustment would have required, because the United States has been the principal victim of the policy of letting its dollar liabilities pile up. Now we are at the stage—and I am really agreeing, you see, with Dr. Rueff on this point— where we are going to have to use the most famous of all adjustment processes, the Procrustean bed; we are going to have to lop off, sooner or later, this excess foreign spending, these excess payments. I am sorry that it has to be done through such a rough process. It would have been much nicer to do it through market forces, not only because that is more in accordance with Adam Smith, which is a good point, but also because market forces, at least theoretically and probably to a large extent in fact, do minimize the cost of adjustment.

But I have to move on because, even though adjustment may be the most important question, our topic is gold and monetary reform. First I must make a slight correction in the excellent summary of my friend, Lionel Robbins. In my great desire to be accommodating, I did agree that we could have an international agreement on the control of future official holdings of dollars. That's as far as I went; I did not agree that we could escape certain inflationary consequences of a massive change in the price of gold.

What, in fact, would be the consequence of a 100 per cent increase in the price of gold? I am not going into the matter of equity, because that is a pragmatic question. The important consideration is what the price increase would do for the world economy. Any benefits to country A or country B are incidental, and I am certainly not concerned with the benefits to the gold producers. They would get nothing extra for the billions in gold they have produced in the past, and if they get anything extra in the future, it would be only because we want the gold.

A 100 per cent increase in the price of gold would raise aggregate reserves of all countries, excluding the International Monetary Fund, by $41 billion. It would do that overnight. We would have to subtract from this figure most of the official holdings of dollars and sterling, on the assumption that the Rueff proposal is adopted, and we would have to add an unknown sum—that is, the return of gold from hoards. Whatever the result, I find this an enormous increase in world reserves on very short notice.

The second point to consider is what would happen to the distribution of reserves. Under the Rueff Plan, the United States would pay off the official holdings of dollars, except for working balances. Its reserves would not increase at all, because the higher price of gold would just cover the debt. If, on top of this, there were a disposition of private dollar holders to say, "We have made a mistake in investment; it is time to cut our losses," and to sell their private dollar holdings to their central banks, that would reduce the reserves of the United States to less than they are today. For the United Kingdom, the outcome would of course be still more unfavorable because, while U.K. gold would be worth $2 billion more than it is today, this gain would be far outweighed by the debt incurred in paying off the sterling balances.

Let us contrast this with what would happen to the countries of Continental Western Europe, which now hold $19 billion of their reserves in gold. These countries would have an increase of $19 billion in the value of their gold holdings; they would of course also get gold for a substantial part—say, $6 billion or $7 billion—of their dollar holdings. To my mind, such an increment of reserves in Western Europe would give us just as bad an imbalance in the distribution of reserves as we had before the United States so generously provided for the reconstitution of Western European reserves by continuing to give billions of dollars in Marshall aid after Western Europe had achieved a balance-of-payments surplus (including, of course, the aid). I don't believe that this proposed new redistribution of reserves could ever be accomplished without a massive inflation in Europe. That is the only way the United States and the United Kingdom could get back some of the enormous increase in Western European reserves.

And as a practical matter, I don't have much faith in the sterilization of the gold profit. I have lived with a real sterilization of gold profit; our profit in 1934 was put into an inactive account that wasn't touched until we got to Bretton Woods, and our money for the International Monetary Fund came from that profit. That kind of sterilization

we could certainly accomplish on paper, but when countries
have such abundant reserves, the very thing will occur that
Dr. Rueff is afraid of; there will be little restraint on running balance-of-payments deficits, because it will be easy to
finance them out of the big increment of reserves gained
from the revaluation of gold.

And now I come to another question: What would the
price increase do for the growth of reserves in the future?
Well, we have Dr. Busschau's testimony. On the growth of
reserves we always have several unknowns. The most
known thing—and even here Dr. Busschau was very cautious—is new production, which can be estimated with reasonable confidence. Other matters are far less clear. Thus,
we don't know what the future flow of gold would be from
the Soviet Union—whether it would be zero or $1 billion a
year. We don't know whether private saving or hoarding of
gold would be on the same or on a smaller scale at the new
price. And we don't know what would happen to industrial
consumption. My own conclusion is that a change of 100 per
cent in the price of gold would involve massive disturbances
of the existing monetary system and generate enormous
uncertainties with which we would have great difficulty in
dealing.

Now I don't want to say that there can't be a change in
the price of gold. But this time I don't think we can handle
the matter by sitting in front of either the pictures in Lord
Robbins' Tate Gallery or those in the Louvre. I think that if
the price of gold is changed, it will come on us through an
inability of the United States to deal with massive conversions of dollars. What will happen then is that the United
States, having paid out large quantities of gold, will say that
it is no longer prepared to make transfers of gold—in either
direction. I honestly believe that if we have a 100 per cent
change in the price of gold, the United States will thereafter
be neither a buyer nor a seller of gold. It will go on the
Meade standard, and other countries can then do business
among themselves with gold if they wish, but if they want to
do business with the United States they will have to buy
dollars with their own currencies in the exchange markets
at such exchange rates as prevail. This may not be the worst
system in the world; I just don't think it's the best.

The advantage of increasing reserves my way is that we

can increase the amount of Reserve Units at a regular rate, at that ideal rate Professor Rueff is seeking but will never find in gold. It can't be done with gold, because there are too many conflicting forces operating on the gold supply. And it is absolutely essential, if we are ever to get to the Exter Plan[2] of no domestic assets in central banks, to have a regular and predictable growth in reserves. I think we can make sure that the growth of reserves is at such a rate that it will never be excessive. I don't want excessive reserves; I would rather err on the side of just a little bit too little.

But I want reserves to grow at an even rate. Mr. Triffin would like to vary the growth from year to year, depending upon whether central banks have created too much domestic credit or too little. In my opinion, the concept that we can arrange reserves for world needs on the basis of national monetary policies is illogical, though it may seem to be ideal. Some countries are always creating too much money and credit; other countries may always be creating too little. Some countries may be creating enough today, too little tomorrow, too much the next day. The notion that we can offset the net effects of what they all do seems to me an illusion. Why, for instance, should it be ideal for a country that has not been creating too much credit to find that world reserves are growing at less than an adequate rate because other countries are pushing their domestic credit expansion too fast?

This is the first big difference between Triffin and me as matters now stand. It is true that if Mr. Triffin, in operating the Triffin Bank, got away from the extension of credit, which I have always called "Triffin I" (maybe unfairly), and if he put more emphasis on the open-market operations, which I have called Triffin II, he would actually be advocating the Reserve Unit system, except that under the Reserve Unit system we know for five years in advance what the creation of Reserve Units will be—say, $1.2 billion a year; and we know how this will be allocated among countries. Professor Triffin wants to leave open the amount he creates each year, each month, or perhaps even each weekend, when the central bankers meet in the picture galleries. My own view is that this is too much management—more than we know how to handle. I think it would be a good thing to

[2] See statement by John Exter, Chapter X, pp. 125–27.

know in advance how much of these Reserve Units are to be created. I don't want to hand over to a group of brilliant technicians, much less bankers, the job of deciding from week to week how much to create in the way of Reserve Units. I want a moderate, regular increase, equivalent to what we would have had if gold production were adequate to the monetary needs of the world.

I also want the reserve increase to be distributed in an assured way among countries. I don't think it will be so overwhelmingly important whether India, for example, gets more Reserve Units under the Fund quota formula than it would under some other formula. If the Indians sell them, they will come into the hands of other countries and India will have received a minor benefit. It will have paid a price by giving up reserves it needs, but it will have obtained import goods in exchange. For the world as a whole, I am satisfied that in this way we can get a proper growth of reserves. In the proposal I have made, we would not retire the dollar and sterling reserves that now exist; we would just add new reserves at a moderate but regular rate.

I regard this as a major part of the practical philosophy of dealing with these problems. I don't want to change the world's monetary system, but to adapt it. First of all, I want to keep gold as reserves. Why get rid of this $41 billion of reserve assets in which the world has such enormous confidence? And I don't want to get rid of the dollar and sterling reserves; but I don't want them to grow, either. In a way, I want to make them into a sort of fixed fiduciary issue in the world's payments system. Mr. Triffin wants to get rid of them. I think that if we do get rid of them *à la* Triffin and Rueff, they will come in through the back door, as Magnifico has so well expounded, through larger holdings of dollars and sterling by commercial banks. But I am keen on not having dollar reserves grow any more (sterling hasn't grown in official holdings, as you know, since 1950). We have to stop the growth of dollars; it is the only way we can keep the dollar equivalent to gold.

Quite simply, I would like the Reserve Unit to be merely that marginal increment which is necessary to give us a steady growth in aggregate reserves at an annual rate of, say, roughly 3 per cent. I want the Reserve Unit also to be a final reserve asset. Call it inconvertible if you wish, though I would like to have it march along with gold so that it would get some of the glitter.

Lord Robbins has asked whether a totally regular growth of Reserve Units would be appropriate in the case of very uneven growth of gold production in the future. Most of the Group of Ten have accepted my suggestion to agree for five-year periods on an appropriate rate of issue of Reserve Units. In any year in which the growth of aggregate reserves has seemed deficient in the previous year, the authorities could then make good the deficiency by a special vote. They would not have to renegotiate each year the amount to add that year; they would negotiate on whether to make the increment a little bit larger or a little bit smaller. If they couldn't agree, we would go on with our steady growth. I should add here that, though gold is a big element in our reserve system, it is not the most variable one. The most variable has been the growth of dollar holdings. Nevertheless, the increment of the world monetary gold stock (including IMF holdings) has varied from zero to $800 million a year in the past sixteen years, and we have to take account of that magnitude of variation. If it should turn out that at this price of $35 an ounce, we can't get any new gold into the world monetary stock, the next five-year agreement would take account of that and a larger amount of Reserve Units would be created.

I have given you some of the differences between Triffin and me—the fancy little things. The biggest difference has been taken away from me. On the biggest difference, I have lost and Triffin has really won. Even though the Group of Ten is discussing the Bernstein Plan and not the Triffin Plan, what they have really done is to adopt—at least in one essential—the Triffin Plan. That is to say, the operation is entrusted, not to a Group of Ten, where you can get enormous responsibility, but to a Group of 105. The Group of Ten are the key countries that Professor John Williams of Harvard came to in his second substitute for the IMF. He started, you will remember, with only the two key currencies—the dollar and sterling. Now that we have agreed upon universal participation, what we really have is a Triffin central bank but with the Bernstein limitation on powers.

I see no need for emphasizing minor differences, so I now come to my final statement. I am not trying to reform the world—to make an ideal international monetary system which will last for 500 or 1,000 years; I am not really interested in this. What I am interested in is to take the problem we have today, which is not at a crisis stage but which could come to the crisis stage, and to find a solution for the problem sufficiently acceptable so that countries will move toward adopting it reasonably promptly. This has always been my approach to these problems. That is why, in 1958, I proposed the General Arrangement to Borrow for the IMF. These borrowing arrangements were very helpful; in their absence, the Fund could not have financed the last British loan. What I am trying to do now with the Reserve Unit proposal is to make sure that the problems of today will be dealt with for a period of fifteen, twenty, or twenty-five years.

I believe that what Triffin wants to do through variations in the rate of growth of reserves could be much better done when a country comes to the Fund to get reserve credit, because what countries will get under my scheme in annual allotments is very small. All the underdeveloped countries together would get $300 million or $400 million a year. The United States would get $300 million a year or less. I don't see how such an annual allotment of reserve units can induce any country to go on with a reckless payments policy. If a country has a reckless policy, it will have to come to the Fund to borrow, and that is where it can and should be disciplined.

I haven't any doubt that my proposal will have to be changed, probably considerably, in the negotiating process. I haven't any doubt that the negotiations will be difficult. But I think we will come to a solution. I think the solution will be along the lines of my proposal, precisely because my plan has a limited scope and a limited objective. Some day, when Triffin is a little older and I am gone from the scene, it would be a pleasure for me to know—up above or down below—that we have taken another step forward from the Bernstein Plan to the Triffin Plan. But not yet. We have at least one more step before we can consider a world central bank.

Robert Triffin

I think we have all agreed—Mr. Rueff, Dr. Bernstein, Dr. Emminger, and myself—on one point brilliantly expressed by Lord Robbins: that the gold-exchange standard has reached its quantitative limit. If there is a nuance of difference on this point, it is theoretical rather than practical. Here I probably feel closer to my friend Jacques Rueff than to Dr. Emminger or Dr. Bernstein, both of whom have commented that the gold-exchange standard has worked relatively well. I agree that it has worked rather well in the postwar period up to, say, 1960 or even up to now—although, as Milton Gilbert has indicated, in the last five years it has not been the old gold-exchange system that has been working but something quite different.

The old gold-exchange standard was based on the idea that central banks were absolutely free to accumulate sterling or dollars, or to convert them into gold at any time they wished. This is no longer true; as Sir Roy Harrod pointed out several years ago, the dollar and sterling have become inconvertible by gentlemen's agreement. And the gold-exchange standard as we knew it was killed, to my mind, by our good friend Bob Roosa, when he had to go around passing the hat and asking people, in the interest of international co-operation, to refrain from exercising the gold-conversion rights upon which the gold-exchange standard was built, so as to avoid a collapse of the system. At that point, the financial or monetary gold-exchange standard was transformed into a political gold-exchange standard. This was unavoidable; I am not against it, but I offer the fact as evidence that the system is no longer working particularly well.

I would also remind you that the gold-exchange standard did not work too well in 1931 and that the consequences of its not working too well were quite fateful and serious for the world. And I would submit that history could repeat itself if we allow the crisis to develop which some of us here fear. I think that even Dr. Bernstein and Dr. Emminger would agree with me that we are in a very precarious situation.

Even when it is working well, the gold-exchange standard introduces two basic sources of disturbance in the long-term working of the international monetary mechanism. First, it makes the annual growth of reserves, which both Dr. Bernstein and I would like to see proceeding at a fairly even pace, extremely haphazard. During the Suez crisis the United States was in surplus, and the total reserves of the world declined. Later the situation reversed: the United States had large deficits, and world reserves increased at a rate that many people regarded as excessive and dangerous. More recently, reserves have stopped growing at all, owing to increasing conversions of dollars into gold.

Second, and even more important, the gold-exchange standard destroys, or transforms in a most unfortunate way, one of the basic features of the old mechanism of adjustment. I am afraid that Dr. Emminger was unfair to Mr. Rueff when he said that it makes no difference whether a country in deficit loses gold or foreign exchange, since in either case it loses reserves and must take remedial measures. While this is true for most countries in the system, it is not true for the reserve-currency countries themselves—*as long as the system works*. When the system worked the United Kingdom and the United States were able to run large deficits without losing much gold or foreign exchange; they simply passed on their IOUs. That feature, of course, changes the picture entirely.

Here I fully agree with Mr. Rueff. But I don't agree with him that this is a very comfortable position for the deficit country. When he tells us that he would order many more suits from his tailor if the tailor were willing to extend credit on indefinite terms, I think he underestimates his own concern for the future. If this famous tailor were to say, "I won't ask you to pay for your suit now; I will not tell you when I will ask you to pay, but I reserve the right—maybe later today, maybe tomorrow, maybe the day after—to demand payment for all the suits you have ordered over the past years," I think Mr. Rueff would worry. And I assure you that the United States has been worried that massive demands for conversion of the IOUs that it has introduced into the world monetary system over the past fifteen years might put it in a very difficult position indeed.

I also find it difficult to agree with Mr. Rueff's contention that a country in deficit which does not benefit from this special favor would always restore its balance-of-payments equilibrium immediately, or within a very short period. After all, only two countries have been favored by the tailor, the United States and the United Kingdom, and I can think of quite a few other countries in recent years which have had serious payments problems lasting many months. Elim-

inating the dollar from the international monetary system is
not going to cure domestic inflation overnight; such problems would still be with us. But I had intended here to stress
my common ground with Mr. Rueff. On the basic point we
are agreed: The gold-exchange standard has come to the end
of the rope, and the system cannot be continued in its present form. This is what Mr. Rueff and I have been saying
for a long time.

We do not, of course, agree on what should be done. Mr.
Rueff would replace the foreign-exchange component of reserves by increasing the gold price. To this proposal various
objections have been made; I would like to repeat some of
them and perhaps make them more precise.

First of all, it seems to me that we all agree with Gardner
Patterson's remark that this involves a very large gamble.
We have to decide all at once what is the magic price that
will assure a reasonable growth of reserves for the next
forty or fifty years, if we are not going to repeat the experience from time to time. I don't know anybody who can say
what that price should be. I have heard many people speak
of a price increase of 50 per cent; many others think the
increase should be 100 per cent, or double the present level.
Our friend Sir Roy Harrod has suggested that the price
should be tripled instead of doubled, and Mr. Schweizer
made a remark here which implied that, to restore the appropriate ratio to the credit superstructure, the price of
gold might have to be multiplied by twenty. I am sure he did
not mean that, but there is a wide range of opinion, and,
frankly, with all my willingness to peer even into a distant
future, I am completely unwilling to predict what price of
gold would give us a golden age for the next fifty years.

As far as quantifying the immediate impact of doubling
the gold price is concerned, however, I would like to repeat
what Dr. Bernstein has said: We give the central banks $41
billion of additional reserves. If—and it is an extraordinarily big "if"—we succeed in negotiating the repayment of the
sterling and dollar balances, as suggested by Mr. Rueff, we
take $23 billion out of those $41 billion. This still leaves $18
billion, to which we should add the $6 billion or so estimated
here for private dishoarding. This would be $24 billion. I
would not like to begin this nice adjustment by pouring
another $24 billion into the system, especially since most of

us are agreed that the present level of reserves—including, of course, the special reserves recently created by bilateral or multilateral negotiation—is more than ample for present needs.

Moreover, whatever the price, the element of haphazardness would remain absolutely untouched. We would have done nothing to assure an orderly and appropriate growth of world reserves. The solution leads into a blind alley. True, it would overcome any danger of a reserve shortage in the near future, and it would solve the problem of lack of confidence in the dollar or sterling. But to think that an appropriate growth of gold reserves in the future would be assured—and, in particular, that it would be assured by changes in the commodity price level—is simply contrary to the historical evidence.

I now come to my final point on raising the gold price. It is true, of course, that with a lot of new international agreements, we could sterilize the effect of too much gold. The banks could sterilize it by reducing the credit component of the system. But I beg you to consider the political and sociological factors involved. We all recognize that it is terribly hard to fight a tendency toward credit inflation. Is it really necessary to add to inflationary pressures by digging deeper holes in South Africa and then to contract credit in order to offset all this? I don't think so. Surely, if it is possible to arrive at a series of complicated agreements about the repayment of U.S. and U.K. debts, about a long-term loan to Britain, and so on, it should be unnecessary to revalue gold. If we can achieve that much co-operation, we can make a fiduciary system à la Bernstein or Triffin work without creating all these problems.

I would now like to comment on my differences with my good friend, teacher, and former boss, Edward Bernstein. I think these differences are even smaller than he has suggested. I, too, have proposed from the very beginning that there should be a presumptive guideline for the regular growth of reserves with, of course, the possibility of correcting that guideline if it appears too steep or not steep enough. My idea has been to specify a ceiling of 3 to 5 per cent in any twelve-month period on the net expansion of the global assets of the system. This ceiling would not necessarily be reached in any given period, particularly in times of inflationary pressures, but it could be exceeded by qualified voting majorities of two-thirds or three-fourths of the total voting power. This ceiling, and the possibility of modifying it, seems very similar to what Dr. Bernstein has suggested, and I don't think it differs at all from the formulation given by Dr. Emminger in the last Group of Ten report. Within these broad limitations, individual loan and investment operations would be designed to support mutually acceptable policies of member countries against temporary balance-of-payments pressures, thus providing a powerful stimulus for the long-run harmonization of member policies and avoidance of unnecessary recourse to exchange restrictions and control.

Actually, I think the only important difference I have with Dr. Bernstein is on this question of the link to adjustment. I would try to aid the adjustment process by providing that the additional purchasing power resulting from an increase in fiduciary reserves be distributed to support adjustment policies of the various member countries. If this is not feasible because people prefer to use a rule of thumb and to decide blindly in advance that whatever is distributed will be distributed according to some arbitrary formula, I am sure that in the long run our two approaches will move toward each other. So if the negotiators find it easier to agree on a flat formula to start the ball rolling, I would not object too much; I am sure it would not remain flat for very long.

Professor Meade has suggested that adjustment would always be a difficult problem, and I agree with him. He thinks we will have to resort to some degree of exchange rate flexibility to solve the problem. I agree there, too, in the sense that I think that for a long time to come we will have to change exchange rates from time to time. I don't agree, however, with the idea of a floating rate, and I would like to explain why. Such a system would introduce a new "ratchet effect" that would not otherwise exist.

Let me cite an example. I like to illustrate with the Dutch, as they are such wise people. But suppose they were to decide tomorrow to distribute 2 billion guilders to the veterans of the last war or to engage in a big credit expansion. Does this mean that Dutch prices and costs would suddenly rise steeply? Not if the exchange rate is stable. The increased purchasing power would spill out into imports from Germany, Belgium, and France, and this would minimize the disturbance to the domestic price structure. On the other hand, if the exchange rate is free to float *à la* Friedman, what would happen? In that case, any domestic monetary mistake, instead of upsetting the balance of payments, would be bottled in; and there would be a very big difference between the bottling-in of inflationary mistakes and the bottling-in of deflationary mistakes. If there were an excessive monetary expansion, there would immediately be a rise in the price of foreign currencies, in import prices, in the cost of living, and, under modern conditions, in wage rates. And once wage rates went up, they would not come down. If, later on, there were a deflationary mistake, it would *not* reduce wage rates—it might reduce employment, but not wage rates—so that there would be a ratchet effect. In other words, any expansionary mistake would be followed by a permanent increase in wage rates and therefore a permanent increase in the domestic price level, while a deflationary mistake would not be followed by a fall in wages and prices.

Professor Meade, however, does not want a fully floating rate; he would like a managed rate. But managed by whom? Who, for example, would manage the dollar-sterling rate—the Bank of England or the Federal Reserve system? And of course this is not just a matter of two countries, as there are a hundred or more countries in the exchange rate structure. I think Professor Meade comes to grips with the logic of his system in suggesting that there should be an international equalization account whereby exchange rate decisions would be taken by the IMF. I won't accuse him of being visionary, as that charge has often been directed at me, but I think that he would be giving the Fund a very difficult assignment.

I agree very much with Dr. Bernstein that reform will have to be gradual and that evolution will unavoidably depend to a large degree on the negotiating process. If you find a door which is locked, you try the next one. I have been suggesting a very simple agreement on gradualism which could, I think, be negotiated much more easily than the agreement we now have in mind about future "contingency planning." Moreover, it would solve the most urgent

immediate problem. For the most urgent problem is not
what will happen to the world when the reserve pool is no
longer fed by American deficits. That problem does not
demand our immediate attention. The main problem facing
us now is the possibility of massive conversion of foreign
exchange into gold. This problem could be taken care of by
the system I have proposed, a gold conversion account,
which would create a new reserve asset—not in order to
expand world reserves but simply to consolidate the existing
reserves. Later, at a second stage, this solution would raise
fewer problems of a political nature when we want to add to
world reserves.

If Dr. Bernstein has moved toward the world-wide Triffin
Plan, I have in a certain sense, and as a first step, moved
back toward the initial Bernstein Plan. My point is that we
should internationalize only the currencies which are in
demand—in other words, buy with international assets only
the currencies which the Fund needs to lend to its members
for use in international settlements. That is to say, we
should internationalize the dollar, sterling, and the currencies of Continental Europe; we should not internationalize
cruzeiros, kips, bahts, or kyats. I think it is absurd to deal
with the problem in the latter way. But I agree that it may
be the only way we will be able to start.

Finally, I have been accused of wanting to go to the moon.
I would be very happy to make the trip in such good company as Dr. Bernstein or as Dr. Emminger, who up to now
has had his feet firmly planted on the Bundesbank's solid
ground, which no one could mistake for the moon's uncertain terrain. The point I would emphasize is this: I fully
recognize that, whether we get to the moon or not, we have
to move gradually. But, whatever the immediate steps we
take, it is extremely important in deciding among the various alternatives to choose approaches that do not lead into
blind alleys, but that are germinal—that have within themselves the potentialities for a viable evolution toward a more
promising future.

*Members of the Bologna Center Conference
on Gold and International Monetary Reform, January 12–15, 1967*

MAURICE ALLAIS, Professor of Economics, Ecole Nationale Supérieure des Mines, Paris

EDWARD M. BERNSTEIN, President, EMB (Ltd.), Washington, D.C.

ARTHUR I. BLOOMFIELD, Professor of Economics, University of Pennsylvania

WEIR M. BROWN, Deputy Permanent Representative, U.S. Mission to the OECD, Paris

WILLIAM J. BUSSCHAU, Chancellor, Rhodes University

ANGUS COLLIE, Secretary General, Gold Study Committee, Chamber of Mines, Johannesburg

PHILIP CORTNEY, Vice Chairman, Monetary Commission, International Chamber of Commerce

DOUGLAS F. DOWD, Professor of Economics, Cornell University

OTMAR EMMINGER, Member, Board of Governors, Deutsche Bundesbank

JOHN EXTER, Senior Vice President, First National City Bank of New York

MILTON GILBERT, Economic Adviser, Bank for International Settlements

CARL HENRY, Economist, New York

RANDALL HINSHAW, Professor of Economics, Claremont Graduate School

JOHN EDWARD HOLLOWAY, Director, South African Board, Barclays Bank, Johannesburg

JACQUES L'HUILLIER, Dean, Faculty of Economics and Social Science, University of Geneva

GIOVANNI MAGNIFICO, Representative, Banca d'Italia in London

RAFFAELE MATTIOLI, President, Banca Commerciale Italiana, Milan

DONALD H. McLAUGHLIN, Chairman, Homestake Mining Company, San Francisco

J. E. MEADE, Professor of Political Economy, Cambridge University

SILVANO MONTANARO, Banca d'Italia, Rome

ROBERT A. MUNDELL, Professor of Economics, University of Chicago

GARDNER PATTERSON, Professor of Economics, Princeton University

Lord ROBBINS, Chairman, *The Financial Times*, London

STUART W. ROBINSON, JR., Economist, Vaud, Switzerland

Sir ERIC ROLL, Fellow, Institute of Politics, Harvard University

JACQUES RUEFF, Chancellor, Institut de France, Paris

EDGAR SALIN, Editor, *Kyklos*, Basle

L. H. SAMUELS, Professor of Economics, University of the Witwatersrand

SAMUEL SCHWEIZER, Chairman, Swiss Bank Corporation, Basle

MICHAEL SPIELER, Financial Adviser, Union Corporation, Ltd., London

WILLARD L. THORP, Chairman, Development Assistance Committee, OECD, Paris

ROBERT TRIFFIN, Pelatiah Perit Professor, Yale University

FRANCESCO VITO, Rector, Catholic University of the Sacred Heart, Milan

JOHN PARKE YOUNG, Visiting Professor of Economics, Claremont Graduate School

NAME INDEX

Allais, Maurice, 3, 134–37, 134n, 148
Anderson, B. M., 12
Bernstein, Edward M., 1, 4, 6, 13, 24, 37, 39, 47, 53–73, 53n, 75–96, 125, 127, 129, 131, 132, 134–35, 137, 139, 143, 147–50, 153, 155, 157–65, 167, 169–71
Busschau, William, J., 6, 109, 109n, 110, 112–15, 133–34, 143–44, 160
Chardin, Teilhard de, 52
Charon, Jean, 52
Cortney, Philip, 138–41, 138n
d'Estaing, Giscard, 47, 51
Dowd, Douglas F., 146
Emminger, Otmar, 39, 48, 89, 95, 97–107, 127–28, 130–31, 135–36, 145, 148, 150, 155, 164–66, 171
Exter, John, 3, 125–27, 125n, 130, 146, 161
Gilbert, Milton, 6, 27–36, 27n, 37, 51, 89, 129, 143–44, 165
Harrod, Sir Roy, 4, 165, 167
Hawtrey, Sir Ralph, 14, 55
Hicks, J. R., 138–39
Hinshaw, Randall, 1–6
Hitler, Adolf, 50
Hume, David, 8–9, 20
Jacobsson, Per, 138–40
Johnson, President Lyndon B., 103, 146
Kennedy, President John F., 103
Keynes, Lord, 13, 82
Lehfeldt, R. A., 55
Lenin, Nikolai, 50
Machlup, Fritz, 48
Magnifico, Giovanni, 127–29, 127n
Marshall, Alfred, 12, 121n
Martin, William McChesney, Jr., 43, 45

McLaughlin, Donald H., 6, 109, 109n, 110–12
Meade, J. E., 3, 5–6, 121–25, 121n, 128–29, 134, 145–47, 151, 160, 169
Morgenthau, Henry, Jr., 155
Mundell, Robert A., 129–32, 129n, 157
Nurkse, Ragnar, 5n
Patterson, Gardner, 132–34, 132n, 144, 150–53, 167
Pigou, A. C., 121n
Ricardo, David, 20
Rist, Charles, 138
Robbins, Lord, 1, 6, 7–23, 7n, 47, 49, 123, 143–50, 157–58, 160, 165
Robertson, D. H., 121n
Roosa, Robert V., 165
Roosevelt, President Franklin D., 37, 41 43–44, 81
Rueff, Jacques, 1, 3, 4, 6, 37–46, 37n, 47, 75–98, 101, 103–4, 109, 125–30, 132–34, 143, 145, 147–48, 150–56, 158, 160, 164–67
Schumpeter, Joseph A., 138
Schweizer, Samuel, 167
Smith, Adam, 158
Spieler, Michael, 6, 109, 109n, 110, 115–19
Stalin, Joseph, 14
Stamp, Max, 23
Thorp, Willard L., 75, 75n, 76, 77, 85, 87, 89, 92, 96, 157
Triffin, Robert, 1, 3, 4, 5–6, 37, 39, 47–52, 47n, 63, 75–96, 124–25, 127, 129, 131–32, 134–35, 137, 143, 145, 147, 148, 150, 153, 155, 164–71
Viner, Jacob, 9
Williams, John H., 16

175

SUBJECT INDEX

Adjustment, international: emphasis on at Bologna Center conference, 3; lack of automatic mechanism for, 8; Hume theory of, 20; Ricardian theory of, 20; and gold-exchange standard, 99; and gold standard, 100–1; under flexible exchange rates, 121–25; under fixed exchange rates, 129–30; postwar performance, 157–58

Allocation of new reserves: Bernstein approach to, 86–90; Triffin approach to, 88–96; via increase in gold price, 105–6; Rueff on Bernstein approach to, 154

Automaticity: Triffin comment on, 79; Rueff view on, 82

Bank of England: domestic assets of, 126; policy of before 1931 crisis, 153–54

Bank of France: domestic assets of, 127

Bernstein approach: basic features of, 63–73; allocation of new reserves under, 86–91; common ground with Triffin approach, 149–50; criteria for reserve growth, 161

Bologna Center conference: purpose of, 1; dialogue among plan authors, 75; emphasis on gold facts, 109, 132

Bretton Woods conference, 12–13, 37, 92

China: gold reserves of, 64

Civil War, U.S., 44

Clearing union: Keynes plan for, 16

Commercial banks; and gold-exchange standard, 127–28

Commitment to maintain gold value of dollar, 103

Common Market countries: net exports as per cent of GNP, 61

Confidence problem under gold-exchange standard, 3, 18

Contingency planning, 28, 30, 170

Criteria for reserve growth: under Bernstein approach, 161–62; under Triffin approach, 161–62

CRU plan, 50, 83–84

Deficit in U.S. balance of payments. *See* U.S. deficit in balance of payments

Deficits without tears, 2, 130

Deflation: under fixed exchange rates, 4; under gold standard, 53

Dishoarding of gold, 80, 114–19, 158–59, 167

Dollar holdings, foreign: and U.S. payments deficit, 27; changes in, 32; need to replace, 41; danger of conversion into gold, 62–63

European Payments Union, 31, 52

Exchange Equalization Fund, U.K., 99, 130

Exchange rates: fixed versus flexible, 4–5, 10–12, 121–25, 134–35, 147; Triffin on flexibility, 169–70

Exter plan, 161

Far East: and gold hoarding, 115–16

Federal Reserve: acquisition of domestic assets, 126–27; recent policies of, 153–54

Flexible exchange rates, 4–5, 10–12, 121–25, 134–35, 147, 169–70

178   SUBJECT INDEX

Foreign exchange: as monetary
reserves, 58–63; variability of
growth as reserves, 64–65
France: dollar holdings of, 32;
conversion of dollar holdings,
40; Rueff illustration, 152
Fundamental disequilibrium, 15

General Arrangements to Borrow,
IMF, 28, 164
Genoa conference, 55
Germany: Meade   illustration,
122;   Magnifico   illustration,
128; Rueff illustration, 152;
Saar negotiations, 155
Gold: hoarding and dishoarding,
2, 64, 80, 114–19, 158–59, 167;
industrial consumption, 2, 81,
109; guaranties, 28, 29, 46; U.S.
purchase of from IMF, 32;
changes in reserve holdings of,
34–35; embargo on, 46, 156;
wishful thinking about, 53; as
fraction of total reserves, 60–
61;   variability   of   reserve
growth, 64; role in future of,
69–73; sterilization of, 159–60
Gold bloc, 55
Gold clause, 46
Gold Delegation, League of Nations, 37, 97
Gold-exchange standard: and confidence problem, 3, 18; and international adjustment, 3, 99; a
"cancer," 38; opposed by Rueff,
77; absurdity of, according to
Rueff, 81; and new reserves, 98,
101; and inflation, 99–100; and
the United Kingdom, 100; and
the United States, 100; at quantitative limit, 145; future of,
145; and U.S. payments deficit,
151–53; never planned, 153;
recent poor performance of,
165; transformed into political
standard, 165
Gold Pool, 29, 104
Gold, price of. See Price of gold
Gold production: and commodity
price level, 38, 78–79; proposal
to control, 55; of United States,
110–12; of free world, 112–14
Gold standard: United States still
on, 38; and price stability, 53–
54; flexibility of, 77; "rules of
the game," 99; and the inter-

national adjustment, 100–1
Gold-tranche position in IMF, 30,
51
Great Britain. See United Kingdom
Great Depression: monetary effects of World War I liquidated
in, 77; and price of gold, 138–
39
Group of Ten: and contingency
planning, 28; reserve position
of, 31; gold holdings of, 34–35;
negotiating process in, 50–51;
lack of agreement in, 52; and
international adjustment, 91;
on reserve growth criteria, 95;
position on adequacy of reserves, 97–98; report of, 98;
and Bernstein approach, 163;
and Triffin approach, 163

Haberler-Pigou effect, 129
Havana conference, 12
Heptarchy, 8
Hoarding, gold, 2, 64, 114–19
Homestake Mine, 111

Incomes policy, 37
India: and gold hoarding, 115–
17
Inflation: as postwar problem, 14;
under gold standard, 53; and
gold-exchange standard, 99–100
International Bank for Reconstruction and Development, 24
International   Monetary   Fund
(IMF): evaluation of role, 12–
18; and gold standard, 14; and
international liquidity, 16; provisions on gold price, 19; as
world central bank, 23; General
Arrangements to Borrow, 28,
164; mitigation procedure, 28;
technical drawings, 28; Ital-
ian special deposit, 29; gold-
tranche position, 30, 51; increase in quotas, 32, 92–93; and
flexible exchange rates, 137
Italy: special deposit with IMF,
29; Magnifico illustration, 128

Jewelry: gold, 115–19; and gold
hoarding, 117

Keynes plan for clearing union, 16

MONETARY REFORM AND THE PRICE OF GOLD
Alternative Approaches

Edited by Randall Hinshaw

Designed by Gerard A. Valerio

Composed by Kingsport Press, Inc., in Linotype Century Expanded

Printed letterpress by Kingsport Press, on 60 lb. Warren's 1854

Bound by Kingsport Press in Holliston Lexotone #31029